50 Companies
That Changed
the World

50 Companies That Changed the World

Incisive Profiles of the 50 Organizations,
Large and Small, That Have Shaped the Course
of Modern Business

by Howard Rothman

CAREER PRESS

Franklin Lakes, NJ

50 Companies That Changed the World
Edited and typeset by John J. O'Sullivan
Cover design by David Fiore
Printed in the U.S.A. by Book-mart Press

To order this title, please call toll-free 1-800-CAREER-1
(NJ and Canada: 201-848-0310) to order using VISA or MasterCard,
or for further information on books from Career Press.

**CAREER
PRESS**

The Career Press, Inc., 3 Tice Road, PO Box 687,
Franklin Lakes, NJ 07417
www.careerpress.com

Library of Congress Cataloging-in-Publication Data

Rothman, Howard.
50 companies that changed the world : incisive profiles of the 50 organizations, large and small, that have shaped the course of modern business / by Howard Rothman.
    p. cm.
Includes index.
ISBN 1-56414-496-8 (cloth)
    1. Organizational effectiveness—Case studies. 2. Organizational effectiveness—United States—Case studies. 3. Success in business—United States. 4. Success in business—United States case studies. I. Title: Fifty companies that changed the world. II. Title.

HD58.9 .R67 2001
338.7—dc21   00-065105

Dedication

This book is dedicated to my family, who changed my world.

Acknowledgments

This book is the product of a great deal of research and many years of observation. Much of what ultimately shaped it, in fact, was transmitted to me in unrelated contexts. In thanking those who assisted in its development, therefore, I find myself reaching back to other books, articles, projects, and conversations that helped to form the initial basis for the selection process along with the analytical thinking that eventually produced *50 Companies That Changed the World*. I also looked back to those direct interviews and suggestions that resulted in the shaping of the words ultimately found on these pages.

Thanks, then, to Ben Cohen, Hass Hassan, Peter Cove, Lee Bowes, Yvon Chouinard, Margot Fraser, John Kirk, Bernie Glassman, Paul Hawken, John Hickenlooper, Bruce Hutton, Wendy Weir, Marilyn Hamilton, Joan Shapiro, Joyce Meskis, Don Banducci, and, as always, Lew Goodman.

I would also like to specifically thank Pat Rothman, Ted Pinkowitz, Ed Epstein, Amy and Carl Boymel, Mary Scott, Leslie Petrovski, John Blakney, Bob Carmel, Louis Morgan, Pam Carson, David Wilbrecht, Barbara Friend, Ellen Kaplan, Robert Butler, Paul Desmond and Ken Tabb for both their general input and pinpoint suggestions; Michael Lewis for offering me the project in the first place; Jackie Michaels and Kirsten Beucler for their publicity and marketing support; John J. O'Sullivan for his editing and design; and the Doors, Steely Dan, the Afro Celtic Sound System, and the Waterboys for providing a soundtrack that helped propel it all.

I am, of course, solely responsible for the contents of this book and for any and all misuses I might have made of the suggestions received from those cited above, and others I have inadvertently failed to mention.

Contents

soft AT&T Ford Apple McDonald's America Online FedEx CBS Philip Morris Wal-Mart Ge
ric IBM Sears Roebuck Motors J.P. Morgan & Co. Union Pacific RCA Nike Intel CNN Boeing He
ard Standard Oil Sony USX-U.S. Steel Group Agence France-Presse Levitt & Sons Walt D
cape Coca-Cola Thyssen Krupp Proctor & Gamble Yahoo! Toyota People Express Manpower Toy
National Football League Kellogg Johnson Publishing Firestone Tire & Rubber Avon Products
Is Ben & Jerry's Homemade RE/MAX Singer Sewing Shorebank Corp. Metro-Goldwyn-Mayer L.L.
Heinz Microsoft AT&T Ford Apple McDonald's America Online FedEx CBS Philip Morris Wal-
ral Electric IBM Sears Roebuck Motors J.P. Morgan & Co. Union Pacific RCA Nike Intel CNN B
ett-Packard Standard Oil Sony USX-U.S. Steel Group Agence France-Presse Levitt & Sons Walt D
cape Coca-Cola Thyssen Krupp Proctor & Gamble Yahoo! Toyota People Express Manpower Toy
National Football League Kellogg Johnson Publishing Firestone Tire & Rubber Avon Products
Is Ben & Jerry's Homemade RE/MAX Singer Sewing Shorebank Corp. Metro-Goldwyn-Mayer L.L.
Heinz Microsoft AT&T Ford Apple McDonald's America Online FedEx CBS Philip Morris Wal-
ral Electric IBM Sears Roebuck Motors J.P. Morgan & Co. Union Pacific RCA Nike Intel CNN B
ett-Packard Standard Oil Sony USX-U.S. Steel Group Agence France-Presse Levitt & Sons Walt D
cape Coca-Cola Thyssen Krupp Proctor & Gam
National Football League Kellogg Johnson Publishing
Is Ben & Jerry's Homemade

Introduction

N o matter how you feel about its individual entities or overall force, the corporate world has a major and ongoing impact on our lives. We work in it. We eat the food it produces and distributes. We drive the cars it manufactures. We communicate over its networks. We house and clothe, entertain and educate ourselves with the various items that it makes. Along the way, this corporate world helps shape what we are even as we—through our feedback and support—help shape what it becomes.

In the following pages, you will read about 50 outstanding companies that have dramatically and permanently altered us. In the process, you will also see how the general structure of business—and, along with it, our society—has evolved over the past few centuries. You will meet some individuals with extraordinary vision, courage, and commitment who struggled to realize their ideas and drive their companies to success. In a very real sense, they are the true forces that have changed our world.

Growing up in a family that worked together to operate a busy retail store and a vending company, I've been more than an observer of the business world all my life. I have participated in it actively since I was barely in high school. I started selling cigarettes and magazines during vacations, using an ancient mechanical coin sorting device every Saturday morning to count the change from our soft drink, coffee, and candy machines. Later, when I became a journalist, I began as a reporter on the business beat for a now defunct urban newspaper. Eventually, I wound up as a contributing editor for several large consumer and trade magazines, primarily covering business.

During that period, I encountered an array of interesting companies that were doing unique and important things. I enjoyed writing about them so much I turned several related projects into books. As a consultant or participant, I was also involved in the development of a number of commercial enterprises—ranging from a stereo dealership, an advertising agency for medical practitioners, a small business accounting firm, and an Internet service provider.

When I started this book, my goal was to look into the various ways that companies like these could change the world and examine the specific ones that have managed to pull off that lofty goal successfully. To find these companies, I began by compiling a list with the naturals, such as Microsoft and Ford. Then, I drew up another with industries that regularly had earth-shaking impact, such as the fields of communications and transportation. I began circulating both to a network of associates and colleagues that represented a broad range of interests. There were high-tech executives and teachers. Public relations professionals and engineers. Business writers and shopkeepers. Salespeople and retired managers. Everyone generously commented on my selections and most helpfully offered a few of their own. New lists were drawn up, recirculated, and refined. Eventually, a solid list of 50 companies surfaced that I felt accurately represented the breadth and scope (if not the totality) of corporate impact on human life in the 19th and 20th centuries.

Then came the researching, writing, and ranking processes. I began by putting the companies into an order that I initially considered appropriate, and started examining a half-dozen of them at a time. Whenever I finished with one I promptly reconsidered its existing rank, especially in relation to the companies that were then immediately above and below it on the list. I constantly asked myself which had more lasting influence, which really deserved to be on top of the other? And, more often than not, this resulted in a change of some sort. For example, I decided after immersing myself in both Philip Morris and Wal-Mart that the former has had more of an impact than the latter, so I flipped the order of the two. I soon began printing out my most current rankings first thing every morning, posting it beside my computer, and then staring at it throughout the day. Few passed without me making at least a tweak or two as the finished chapters started piling up and my knowledge of all the companies increased. Several times I also deleted companies that I had originally targeted. After examining them fuller, I no longer felt that they honestly belonged. At last, when an initial draft was finished, I circulated the final list among many of my original confidants. Most agreed with the new lineup, but a few suggested additional changes. Several of those were incorporated into the ranking that the finished book contains.

The profiles themselves, read in order or otherwise, offer insight into the often forgotten details of our various cultural metamorphoses as directed by these leading businesses. For example, you will see how our means of transportation were transformed from trains and cars to airplanes and rockets. How the communications evolution took us from newspapers, to radio, to TV, to cyberspace. How we underwent a social conversion through the introduction of electricity and telephones, chain hotels and fast-food joints. The overall picture is one of business and societal alchemy at the hands of a few farsighted people, whose best ideas were usually copied and ultimately adapted into the mainstream. But the individual pictures are even more fascinating, for they show precisely how these leading firms managed to stay atop their changing worlds by following a singular focus, but altering direction as necessary whenever it proved critical.

It isn't surprising, therefore, to learn that virtually all of the companies in this book, no matter when or where they were founded, still make a big impact on who we are and what we do. I wrote this book, for example, on an **Apple** computer with the assistance of a **Netscape** browser, **Microsoft** word processing software and **Hewlett-Packard** printer. During the process I purchased a card table and chairs from **Wal-Mart**, and a lawnmower from **Sears**. I got **FedEx** deliveries about three times a week, and regularly watched **CNN, CBS**, and the **National Football League** on my cable connection from **AT&T**. My very first car was from **General Motors** (1959 Chevy Impalla), my next car was a **Toyota** (1974 Celica GT), and my current car runs on **Firestone** tires (although, thankfully, not a model that the company recalled in the summer of 2000). I exercise in **Nike** footwear, unwind with a **Sony** CD player, take my kids to practically every movie released by the **Walt Disney Company**, and when they were younger felt that I lived at **Toys "R" Us**. When my wife and I first met, her roommate was engaged to a guy from **Levittown**. I flew **People Express** for the few years we could. Today, I have products at home too numerous to mention from **Kellogg, Procter & Gamble, Phillip Morris, H.J. Heinz, L.L. Bean, Coca-Cola**, and of course, **Ben & Jerry's**. The most unusual connection of all, however, came when I discovered that the scientist who founded a company responsible for both **GE** and **RCA** began his career as a chemistry teacher at the Philadelphia high school I attended a century later.

What's the point? These "50 companies that changed the world" obviously all made a tremendous mark on the business world, initiating such vital operational innovations as the assembly line, franchising agreement, brand extension, and temporary employee. At the same time, they made perhaps an even larger mark on the world in general, and on each and every one of us.

There have also been negative impacts, as evidenced by giant tobacco company-cum-consumer products conglomerate Phillip Morris and wartime armsmaker turned peacetime steelmaker Thyssen Krupp. However, these firms and their visionaries, while rarely setting out to change the world, usually did so in a very positive manner.

And while practically all of them still battle challenges consistently in order to remain on that influential edge, most have faced down similar threats successfully throughout their existence. That's one of the primary reasons they are included in this book. It is my hope that their stories will prove to be both instructive and interesting to all.

A final note: Several people who have read this book have asked about the possibility of investing in one or more of these companies. Over the years, this has generally been a smart move. Several of them are longtime components of the Dow Jones Industrial Average, and others have been leaders on the NASDAQ exchange during the tech boom. With the market instability during the latter half of 2000, however, even these standard-bearers have taken their hits. Companies such as Microsoft, AT&T, and Ford have not been immune to the fluctuations in stock valuation that have hit most market segments. Nonetheless, long-term investors can take some comfort in the fact that the companies described here are clearly established and generally profitable. All have a decent chance of rebounding with the economy in a stronger position than their peers. Betting on their future success is obviously no sure thing, but if their past history is any indication they certainly should be expected to hold their own in the years to come.

Howard Rothman
Centennial, Colorado
January, 2001

osoft AT&T Ford Apple McDonald's America Online FedEx CBS Philip Morris Wal-Mart Gt
tric IBM Sears Roebuck Motors J.P. Morgan & Co. Union Pacific RCA Nike Intel CNN Boeing He
kard Standard Oil Sony USX-U.S. Steel Group Agence France-Presse Levitt & Sons Walt C
scape Coca-Cola Thyssen Krupp Proctor & Gamble Yahoo! Toyota People Express Manpower Toy
National Football League Kellogg Johnson Publishing Firestone Tire & Rubber Avon Products
is Ben & Jerry's Homemade RE/MAX Singer Sewing Shorebank Corp. Metro-Goldwyn-Mayer L.L.
Heinz Microsoft AT&T Ford Apple McDonald's America Online FedEx CBS Philip Morris Wal
eral Electric IBM Sears Roebuck Motors J.P. Morgan & Co. Union Pacific RCA Nike Intel CNN B
lett-Packard Standard Oil Sony USX-U.S. Steel Group Agence France-Presse Levitt & Sons Walt C
scape Coca-Cola Thyssen Krupp Proctor & Gamble Yahoo! Toyota People Express Manpower Toy
National Fo ll League Kellogg Johnson Publishing Firestone Tire & Rubber Avon Products
is Ben omemade RE/MAX Singer Sewing Shorebank Corp. Metro-Goldwyn-Mayer L.L.
Heinz Microsoft AT&T Ford Apple McDonald's America Online FedEx CBS Philip Morris Wal
eral Electric IBM Sears Roebuck Motors J.P. Morgan & Co. Union Pacific RCA Nike Intel CNN B
lett-Packard Sta Sony USX-U.S. Steel G Agence France-Presse Levitt & Sons Walt C
scape Coca-Col er Toy
National Football League Kellogg Johnson Publishing Firestone Tire & Rubber Avon Products
is Ben & Jerry's Homemade

Number 1

Microsoft Corporation

Fact File:

✓ Founders: William H. Gates III and Paul Allen
✓ Distinction: Created the systems that drive nearly all the world's PCs.
✓ Primary products: Computer software and Internet services.
✓ Annual sales: $22.956 billion.
✓ Number of employees: 31,400.
✓ Major competitors: America Online, Oracle, Sun Microsystems.
✓ Chairman and Chief Software Architect: William H. Gates III; President and CEO: Steven A. Ballmer.
✓ Headquarters: Redmond, Wash.
✓ Year founded: 1975.
✓ Web site: www.microsoft.com.

You may love them or hate them, but there's no denying them: Microsoft is currently the world's most powerful company. Founded 25 years ago by two boyhood friends, the corporation grew up with the personal computer. Microsoft is neither the largest on Earth nor the most valuable. It doesn't set the pace for technical innovations or employee relations. It isn't sexy like a dotcom, seductive like a sports franchise, or alluring like an entertainment concern. What it is, though, is the purveyor of the software that runs 90 percent of all PCs—and that gives it a dominance that no other company, inside its industry or out, can match.

Starting in 1975, when Bill Gates and Paul Allen translated an existing mainframe computer programming language into one that could be used with the very first PC, the company they christened with a combination of the words "microcomputer" and "software" has been uncannily successful. It soared from $16,000 in revenues in its first year to $7.5 million in its fifth. It went global, forged critical partnerships with all of the leading computer makers, vastly expanded its product line, and was earning nearly $150 million annually by its 10th anniversary. Then, it went public—making Gates the youngest billionaire in U.S. history, and eventually the richest person in the world—while consistently tallying an astounding 25 cents in profit on every dollar it earned.

But with those accomplishments, Microsoft also has been unceasingly controversial. It has been faulted for taking innovations developed by others and turning them to its own commercial advantage. For leveraging its enormous power to stifle competition and force consumers into costly upgrades. For missing the onset of the Internet boom and then trying to bludgeon its way into the fray. For all these things and for making much more money and lasting far longer than anyone in its field, the company had been in the critical crosshairs since its beginning.

And then, in mid-1998, the U.S. Department of Justice and a coalition of 20 state attorneys general officially accused it of violating antitrust laws—a charge that ultimately led to an order that the company be split in two. With the case in lengthy legal limbo, however, Microsoft adamantly dug in its heels to retain the tremendous power it had amassed.

Paul Allen saw the future in 1975 when he picked up a copy of *Popular Mechanics* with the MITS Altair on its cover. Allen, then working at Honeywell, instantly understood that this primitive device would completely change the way computers were used. He showed the magazine to long-time friend Bill Gates, a fellow Seattle native and Harvard sophomore. Gates wrote his first computer program and started his first computer-related business when barely in his teens. Gates grew equally excited with the possibilities, and the two immediately began working round-the-clock to adapt the popular BASIC programming language used on large computers for this new personal-sized machine.

Allen flew to MITS headquarters in Albuquerque to demonstrate their effort as soon as it was completed, and it so impressed the company they offered him a job. He also began actively promoting the new Altair BASIC, which attracted the attention of hobbyists who had longed for such an innovation. Gates got caught up in the enthusiasm as well, and dropped out of Harvard to follow his friend to New Mexico. There, the two struck up an informal partnership they called Micro-soft—with a hyphen to emphasize the corporate origins—and began refining their creation. That first year, it took in $16,005.

The two opened offices in Albuquerque and licensed their program to several large firms, including General Electric and NCR. Both were attracted by the Altair buzz. They hired employees to meet ensuing demand, and in 1977 formalized the company's existence. Gates also began speaking out against hobbyists who were pirating their product, incurring the wrath of those who believed that such programs should be freely traded. It would not, of course, be the last time Gates and his company were accused of imposing their will on the computer world.

More licenses for BASIC were quickly negotiated, including those for the recently unveiled Commodore PET and TRS-80 computers (along with an upstart from northern California called Apple). By the end of 1977 Microsoft also began shipping a second computer language, FORTRAN, and selling BASIC on a single-copy basis. When revenues neared $400,000, Gates and Allen decided to move their headquarters to Bellevue, Wash.

After striking a deal with a Japanese firm to begin marketing BASIC overseas, Microsoft's business began to accelerate. And then, just before its fifth anniversary, the company signed a seminal contract with IBM to produce the operating system for its own soon-to-be-unveiled personal computer. Microsoft—now with 40 employees, including a young executive named Steve Ballmer who had recently arrived from Procter & Gamble—had nothing of the kind under development. So Gates bought a program called QDOS (which stood for Quick and Dirty Operating System) from Seattle Computer Products for $50,000. His firm then adapted it to meet IBM's needs, renamed it MS-DOS (for Microsoft's Disk Operating System), and wound up in exactly the right place with the right product when sales of the IBM-PC exploded upon its 1981 release. Revenues hit $16 million and the employee base was tripled to meet demand.

In the 16 months after it was first offered, the company licensed its MS-DOS to 50 more hardware manufacturers, and Microsoft really took off. It opened offices in Europe, while using its increasing income to produce an electronic spreadsheet and move into the growing market for business software. Co-founder Allen left the company in 1983 due to illness, and the developments he pioneered continued. They culminated in Microsoft's 10th year, when it shipped its first version of a graphical operating system, named Windows. Sales were initially slow—due in part to the lack of available software—but criticism was strong. Skeptics pointed out that Apple's Macintosh already did everything Windows could do, but better. However, Microsoft continued working to improve it, and business picked up in other areas. Annual revenues soon reached $150 million and the payroll approached 1,000.

The company responded in 1986 by going public and moving into a new four-building campus in Redmond, Wash. Gates, its largest individual shareholder, became a billionaire at age 31. But as his wealth grew and the company's power increased, so did the complaints against it. Rivals regularly accused Microsoft of being underhanded schemers out to profit from every computer sale in the world. Supporters also were growing in number as Microsoft enlarged its reach, however, and they vigorously applauded the improved products that made their computers more effective and efficient.

The late 1980s saw rapidly continuing advances from Microsoft. They introduced a "bundled" suite of applications called Office, CD-ROM products such as the Bookshelf reference collection. And as international operations tallied more than half of all sales Microsoft became the industry's top software vender. Apple sued for copyright infringement. The folks in Redmond seemed unconcerned and expanded their headquarters to accomodate even more employees.

The biggest breakthrough of all came in 1990 when the most refined update yet of the graphical operating system, dubbed Windows 3.0, was released. Microsoft believed it would change the world of personal computing forever, and launched it with a $100 million advertising campaign. The effort appeared justified when unit sales hit 100,000 within two weeks, making the company the first in its industry to surpass $1 billion in sales. The impressive landmark was reached as Microsoft was celebrating its 15th anniversary. It also arrived just a little before the federal government revealed that it was investigating the company for possible antitrust violations.

Microsoft's successes, and the protests leveled its way, multiplied during the 1990s. Millions registered to use Windows in dozens of countries as updates became available, new software was released for home and business use, and a judge ruled in Microsoft's favor in the Apple copyright suit after 63 months of litigation. Rivals, however, increasingly complained about its practices even after a 1994 settlement with the U.S. Justice Department led to the changing of some controversial practices.

The company marked its 20th birthday with the release of Windows 95—which finally matched the ease-of-use of Apple's operating system. More than 4 million copies were sold in four days. Microsoft bundled its new Internet Explorer browser in this version to belatedly counter competitor Netscape in the increasingly hot battlefield of cyberspace. They launched The Microsoft Network online service to grab market share from leader America Online. Gates redoubled his efforts on Internet-related software, but his progress brought even more governmental scrutiny on the firm. And in 1997, the Justice Department officially alleged that Microsoft had violated its three-year-old settlement by compelling manufacturers to include certain products in their computers or risk losing the Windows operating system.

Steve Ballmer was elevated to company president and CEO as Gates assumed the titles of Chief Software Architect and chairman as the federal action continued. In 1999, a judge ruled Microsoft had indeed harmed consumers by violating antitrust laws in its dealings with business partners. The following year, it was ordered to be split into two separate companies; one to handle operating systems and another applications. The company protested vehemently, and in the fall of 2000 the U.S. Supreme Court declared a lengthy appeals process must be undertaken before any resolution was determined.

Observers predicted the decision on whether Microsoft would be dismantled was thus years away. And Gates, the world's richest person and head of its most powerful company, hunkered down to make his firm even more earth-shaking as the 21st century unfolded.

AT&T Corporation

Fact File:

✓ Founders: Alexander Graham Bell, Gardiner Hubbard, and Thomas Sanders.
✓ Distinction: Launched the telecommunications revolution.
✓ Primary products: Telephone services, Internet access, cable television.
✓ Annual sales: $62.391 billion.
✓ Number of employees: 148,000.
✓ Major competitors: America Online, MCI WorldCom, Sprint.
✓ Chairman and CEO: C. Michael Armstrong.
✓ Headquarters: New York, N.Y.
✓ Year Founded: 1877.
✓ Web site: www.att.com.

Advanced communication techniques are widely considered a hallmark of an advanced society. And no corporation is more responsible for the state of that art in today's world than AT&T. The ubiquitous phone company has always been in the forefront of every development in this increasingly vital and complex business—from its first incarnation following Alexander Graham Bell's first telephone in the late 19th century through its ultimate overhaul after a government-mandated divestiture near the end of the 20th century. And when the resultant corporation voluntarily dismantled itself yet again a dozen years later, it prepared to make its mark in the 21st century as well.

American Telephone and Telegraph was once the parent company of the legally sanctioned monopoly known as Ma Bell, and it grew to mammoth proportions, while providing the United States with the best phone service in the world. But its unique

efforts and production facilities overseas, where the company became quickly entrenched and now sells a mind-boggling 76 brands ranging from the most popular at home (Virginia Slims, Merit and Marlboro, among them) to those with exotic and strikingly familiar names (such as Apollo Soyuz, Le Mans and Colorado).

The biggest diversification of all, however, took the tobacco companies into other fields entirely. Philip Morris broadened its portfolio by purchasing the century-old Miller Brewing Company. They owned the rights to a regional low-calorie beer that seemed a natural for invigorating the underperforming brand. The retagged Miller Lite went national in the early 1970s, and with help from popular TV ads starring self-deprecating retired athletes (who loudly argued whether the beer was better because it "tastes great," or because it was "less filling"), it soon captured the number-one spot in this hot new beverage category. By then employing marketing twists used in the cigarette business—adding brand extensions such as "regular" and "draft"—Philip Morris propelled Miller to second-place among U.S. brewers.

The next big change took place soon after, when the company acquired General Foods and Kraft. Kraft Foods has successfully contributed a powerful litany of venerable household names to the corporate effort. These run the gamut from Sanka and Shredded Wheat, to Jell-O and Cool Whip. Not all diversification attempts were as successful, to be sure, with the most prominent failure being the $520 million acquisition of 7-up in 1978. (It was sold at a small loss less than a decade later, when Philip Morris realized that it had paid too much to ever make it work.)

Its beleaguered tobacco business also appeared to be withstanding the onslaught of opponents, who by now had engineered spot bans on smoking in public places. Cigarette sales may have dropped throughout the industry, but they rose at Philip Morris. The company also increased its overseas ventures, and topped rival R.J. Reynolds to become the biggest in the business. But even this master of consumer marketing couldn't successfully fend off all the lawsuits, aggressively battle all the proposed taxes, and perpetually deflect antismoking sentiment. And so, by the 1990s, it was considered something of a pariah. Its stock stagnated and its image was constantly under siege.

Knowledgeable observers nonetheless remained impressed by the way it was handling its unique situation. The company lowered cigarette prices sharply in 1993 to match the discount brands which had suddenly become popular. It vigorously denied smoking's dangers, repeatedly lodged court challenges against regulatory efforts, and enthusiastically aided all efforts to protest proposed cigarette-tax hikes. It also broadened its support for worthy causes—ranging from education reform to the arts. And America's seventh-largest industrial enterprise, with sales of $60.9 billion, looked like it just might weather the storm. "Don't underestimate the champ," *Forbes* magazine proclaimed in a 1993 cover story.

And then, the very next year, a congressional subcommittee revealed a memo written a decade earlier by a Philip Morris researcher who confirmed what everyone else already acknowledged: That nicotine was addictive. Because the company had always steadfastly rejected this view, and vehemently denied that its officials knew of any evidence to the contrary, "the champ" found itself once again on the ropes.

Only one in four Americans now smoke, half the percentage of 40 years ago. In addition, strong restrictions on the marketing, retailing, and use of cigarettes across the United States has demanded innovative response. But make no mistake: The tobacco business remains very lucrative. Philip Morris stock is still languishing at multiples lower than comparable non-tobacco firms—in part because of more than 600 lawsuits now pending against it—and its domestic opportunities to increase market shares are practically nil. But the company managed to hike prices 32 percent in 1999 while demand dropped just 8 percent, and it has been boosting overseas efforts with deals in formerly unconquered territories such as Hungary, Lithuania, and China.

Although cigarettes at home and abroad remain responsible for the lion's share of its overall business, Philip Morris is counting on its food and beverage divisions to produce a bigger chunk of the total pie in years to come. At the turn of the century, about 40 percent of the company's total sales and one-third of its overall profits came from these areas. To boost those shares, it has eliminated jobs, closed plants, and cut prices. Results in the food industry initially proved more positive than those in the beer market. But both of these remain fluid and expectations remain strong.

It is with cigarettes, though, that the fate of Philip Morris has always hung—and, most likely, always will. Tarnished by mounting scientific evidence and growing public scorn, it finally conceded (on its Web site) that there is "overwhelming medical consensus that smoking causes diseases." It outlined what it was doing to help steer youngsters away from the habit, and unveiled new products (such as a cigarette that doesn't start fires if dropped.) Most surprising, it also announced that it would no longer oppose government regulations. Some observers took this news as a positive sign; others were more skeptical. But most thought it meant that Philip Morris was still a long way from throwing in the towel, even if the company name was no longer considered "cool."

10

Wal-Mart Stores Inc.

Fact File:

✓ Founder: Sam Walton.
✓ Distinction: Parlayed retailing innovations into worldwide dominance.
✓ Primary products: Softgoods, hardgoods, electronics, groceries.
✓ Annual sales: $165.013 billion.
✓ Number of employees: 1,140,000.
✓ Major competitors: Costco Wholesale, Kmart, Target.
✓ Chairman: S. Robson Walton; Chairman of the Executive Committee: David D. Glass; CEO and President: H. Lee Scott Jr.
✓ Headquarters: Bentonville, Ark.
✓ Year founded: 1962.
✓ Web site: www.wal-mart.com.

On a crisp fall day in 1983, just about all of the 9,300 residents of Bentonville, Ark., turned out to toast the neighbors who made good. It was Sam and Helen Walton Appreciation Day. A rousing parade with bands and floats had been organized to honor the locals who changed the course of retailing—and the town they called home. Portraits of the couple were everywhere. The newspaper printed a special souvenir edition. President Reagan phoned to offer congratulations. And the Waltons happily soaked it all up from a reviewing stand on Main Street, directly across from the site where they opened a five-and-dime store in 1950.

Things, of course, had gone rather well during the ensuing three decades for Sam Walton and the Wal-Mart discount chain he later founded from this spot in the Ozarks. He was already considered the king of retail. And in just two years, *Forbes* magazine would declare him America's richest man.

But the start of Wal-Mart may have caused Walton to wonder whether he had indeed chosen the proper career path. The very same year he broke ground on his first Wal-Mart Discount City in Rogers, Ark., three other major chains—Kmart, Woolco and Target—also opened their doors. And when Walton launched his second store in nearby Harrison, two truckloads of promotional watermelons that were spread along the sidewalk exploded ominously in the summer heat.

Still, Walton persevered and his vision proved a winner long before his death in 1992 at age 74. By the turn of the century, his company was selling everything from sporting goods and apparel to auto accessories and groceries. Its three types of stores (traditional discounters, superstores, and membership warehouses) were omnipresent across the globe, with some 4,000 operating in all 50 states and nine countries from Canada to China. Along with a fledgling Web site with tremendous potential, the combination solidly cemented Wal-Mart's position as the world's number-one retailer.

While some critics have blasted it for destroying small mom-and-pop stores, Wal-Mart has nonetheless done much to benefit neighbors and employees. And, for better or worse, it has certainly changed the face of retailing.

It seems that Samuel Moore Walton always was destined for greatness. The son of a farm-mortgage broker, he was the youngest Eagle Scout ever in his native Missouri. He also president of his high school student council, as well as quarterback of its state-champion football team. As a young boy he dreamed of becoming U.S. president, and as a teenager yearned to seek an M.B.A. from the prestigious Wharton School. Economic realities got in the way, however, and three days after his 1940 graduation from the University of Missouri he accepted a management trainee position at a J.C. Penney store in Des Moines, Iowa.

The work was hard and the salary was just $75 a month. But the challenge and potential convinced Walton from the start that business in general—and retailing in particular—was the key to his future. He became even more confident of that when the chain's founder, James Cash Penney, dropped in one day and personally taught the young man how to tie an appealing package with minimal twine and paper. The dual lessons of hands-on management and corporate frugality impressed Walton greatly. These lessons would stay with him for the rest of his life.

Walton left the business world briefly for a stint in the Army. Upon his release in 1945, he bought a Ben Franklin variety store in Newport, Ark. (He wanted to open in St. Louis, he said later, but Helen wouldn't move to a town with more than 10,000 residents.) Walton quickly became the consummate small-town merchant, catering to his neighbors' specific tastes and needs. At the same time, he began seeking out sources around the region who offered these goods at prices lower than his official suppliers. After working in the store all day, he would hitch a trailer to his car and drive across the state line into Tennessee and Missouri in search of the products desired by his customers. He'd then price them as cheaply as possible and quickly sell out his entire inventory.

Walton, of course, had discovered the essence of discounting: by cutting prices, sales increased and profits soared. The folks at Ben Franklin didn't like it, but customers certainly did. In less than five years, Walton's store had become a huge success. His landlord, however, decided that it would make a perfect business for his own son. He refused to renew the store's lease. Walton—who had no place else to move in the tiny town—was forced to sell out and start fresh somewhere else. He settled on the even smaller Bentonville, he noted in his memoirs, because it offered access to the hunting seasons in four states.

Around this time he read of two "self-service" discount stores in Minnesota, and decided after visiting them that his new Bentonville shop should also feature open merchandise racks with checkout registers at the front. He called it "Walton's Five and Dime," and promoted it with specials, such as a dozen clothespins for 9 cents. Eager customers came from day one, and kept coming every day after that.

By 1960, Walton and his younger brother, James L. "Bud" Walton, owned 15 such stores tallying $1.4 million in total annual sales. But Mr. Sam, as he liked to be called, wasn't satisfied and began considering new ways to expand. He found one in the massive discount stores cropping up in urban areas from coast to coast, which were selling more types of items at lower prices than any of their competitors. When one encroached on his Arkansas territory, Walton knew he had to act. And on July 2, 1962—at the age of 44—he opened Wal-Mart No. 1 in Rogers.

Everyone thought Walton's dream of bringing the discount concept to small rural towns was crazy. He and Helen were forced to co-sign all the loan notes, pledging their home and property as security. But the idea caught on. Within five years he had 19 such stores, including one in his old haunt of Newport (where the landlord's son's Ben Franklin had since closed). By contrast, Kmart opened in 250 locations during the same period. It steadfastly ignored towns with populations under 50,000, which gave Wal-Mart free rein to exploit its chosen niche.

Walton focused on utilizing everything he had learned over the past two decades. Each store catered to local tastes and featured locally made goods. All honored hometown achievements and supported neighborhood charities. Employees were called "associates" and offered generous profit-sharing plans. Shoppers were personally greeted upon arrival. Building designs were minimal; product variety was paramount. And, most importantly, prices were the absolute lowest they could be. The combination helped Wal-Mart flourish. And in 1970, it went public.

The subsequent cash influx pushed the company's growth into high gear. It funded a self-contained ordering and distribution system, which helped serve the increasingly out-of-the-way locations that traditional suppliers wouldn't touch. It also made the founders very rich, but didn't alter their values or plans one bit. Like his former boss James Cash Penney, Walton strove to visit every store at least once a year. And even though he bought airplanes to do so (he piloted them himself), he still drove around Bentonville in a Ford pickup. "What am I supposed to haul my dogs around in, a Rolls-Royce?" he once asked.

By the 1980s, Wal-Mart began implementing a computerized sales and inventory system that made it even more efficient. It quickly became the envy of the retail industry. Through it all, Walton remained in close touch with every facet of his burgeoning operation. He would still don a Wal-Mart cap and name tag and travel from store to store, pumping up associates with his famous cheer (Give me a W... Give me an A...) and questioning them on prices and sales percentages. If a competitor opened nearby, he would slip off the cap and name tag and anonymously check it out. Often, he would treat hourly employees to lunch. And he once took dozens of donuts to a distribution center at 2:30 a.m., so he could pick the brains of night workers on the loading dock.

Walton was first listed as America's richest man in 1985. However, he hated the tag so much he distributed his billions among family members to shed it. The only thing that proved beyond his indefatigable spirit, in fact, was the bone cancer that eventually felled him less than one month after President Bush gave him the Presidential Medal of Freedom. Bush called him "an American original who embodied the entrepreneurial spirit and epitomized the American dream."

David Glass had replaced Walton as CEO four years earlier. Before accepting his current position as chairman of the executive committee at the start of 2000, Glass infused the company with renewed energy by adding hundreds of supercenters (which combine full-line groceries with the discount stores). He also expanded the Sam's Club membership-only warehouse concept initiated in 1983. He cemented Wal-Mart's position as the number-two company in the *Fortune* 500 by expanding internationally. It is now the top retailer in Canada and Mexico, as well as the United States.

Wal-Mart's impressive success, though, really continues because it still closely follows the tenets originally laid out by its legendary founder.

11

General Electric Company

Fact File:

✓ Founder: Thomas A. Edison.
✓ Distinction: It lit up our lives.
✓ Primary products: Electrical equipment, home applicances, jet engines, financial services, broadcasting.
✓ Annual sales: $110.832 billion.
✓ Number of employees: 340,000.
✓ Major competitors: Matsushita, Rolls-Royce, Siemens.
✓ Chairman and CEO: John F. Welch Jr.
✓ Headquarters: Fairfield, Conn.
✓ Year founded: 1892.
✓ Web site: www.ge.com.

Less than a year before he was scheduled to step down as head of General Electric, Jack Welch signed the most lucrative non-fiction book contract ever awarded. The fabled chairman and CEO, called "the leading management revolutionary of the century" by Fortune magazine, was given an astounding $7.1 million to share his story with the world. That was far more than other business leaders had received for similar projects. It was also more than the amount paid for any previous big-name autobiography, including those written by General Colin Powell, and Pope John Paul II. (This advance was eclipsed in 2001 by the $8 million given to Hillary Rodham Clinton to pen her memoirs.)

Many observers, even some who readily acknowledge Welch as a bona fide business genius, expressed doubt that he could ever peddle enough copies to justify that type of advance. But Welch repeatedly faced such skepticism after taking over at GE in 1981 as the youngest leader in the company's long and storied history. He always found ways to dispel it over the ensuing two decades, and his supporters were confident he could do so once more.

General Electric, to be sure, was already one powerful company when the 45-year-old son of a railroad conductor took control. The year before, it reveled in a $12 billion market value and recorded earnings of $1.5 billion on sales of $25 billion. It could trace its roots to the great Thomas Alva Edison, and notable alumni ranged from Hewlett-Packard co-founder David Packard to offbeat novelist Kurt Vonnegut. It had a hand in developing everything from light bulbs and toaster ovens to televisions and jet planes. Its name was one of the most well-known on Earth.

Welch and his backers felt GE could do better, however, and under his direction it has. By emphasizing quality in both products and processes, the company's sales increased nearly ten-fold while its stock moved consistently upward. Unproductive subsidiaries were jettisoned and promising new ones acquired. A bloated payroll was trimmed drastically and unnecessary layers of bureaucracy cut. In the process, GE was transformed from a successful if lumbering old-line industrial giant into a sleek money-minting conglomerate that now combines manufacturing with service and technology in a way that meshes perfectly for today's global economy.

GE's story begins in 1878, when Thomas Edison founded the Edison Electric Light Company to support his development of a practical incandescent lamp. He produced his first one, along with his first "dynamo," within a year. As other products followed, he renamed the company Edison General Electric. Competing firms started surfacing. One, the Thomson-Houston Electric Company, grew particularly strong because of a series of mergers and acquisitions. Edison ultimately combined forces with it in 1892, and a powerful new entity dubbed General Electric was born.

Through his patents and consulting responsibilities, Edison remained involved with his old company for several years. During this time it moved into various related endeavors—such as building the world's largest electric locomotives and transformers. Success in these fields led to GE's listing in the original Dow Jones Industrial Index in 1896. Today, it is the only one of those initial entries still included.

Edison's passion for invention also rubbed off on his peers. In 1900 the company established a novel research and development center run by Dr. Willis R. Whitney. Over the years GE's in-house scientists developed many trailblazing ideas at this facility in Schenectady, N.Y. (which is now the world's largest private lab of its kind). Among the many early products that took shape here was the first electrically-propelled ship developed for the U.S. Navy in 1912, and the first hermetically-sealed domestic refrigerator unveiled in 1925.

The 1920s additionally kicked off a lengthy period in which General Electric began focusing on the creation of TVs and radios. The company's first connection to this burgeoning news-and-entertainment arena can be traced to 1919, when it helped

David Sarnoff found the RCA Corporation. Its initial intention was to corner as large a portion as possible of the rapidly growing market for radio receivers, which soared in sales from 12 million in 1921 to 207 million in 1926. But during this time, GE also entered the broadcast fray, putting Schenectady's WGY on the air in 1922 in direct competition with RCA's own content providers.

As RCA organized the NBC network and began experimenting with an even more promising media called television—both as a broadcaster and a set producer—GE formed a plastics division to advance development of TV receivers and related products. It also moved into the production of airplane engines as World War II began. In 1942, its turbos powered the very first jet-propelled planes designed and built in the United States. A decade later, its J-79 jet engines were the first to transport aircrafts at twice the speed of sound. The smaller appliances, such as those it had become known for in the past were not neglected. In the 1950s, GE began building early computers (again with RCA) while its housewares division introduced the Toast-R-Oven, along with a clothes dryer that featured the industry's first automatic termination device.

During the next few years General Electric played a role in the creation of even more technically advanced projects, such as the weather satellite and vacuum circuit breaker. And in 1969, it assisted in the Apollo moon landing—which was the result of 37 separate GE operations handled by 6,000 company employees. Dr. Ivar Giaever of its R&D Center was awarded the Nobel Prize for physics in 1973, and the facility designed a critical component for the CAT scanner in 1975. Its lighting division by this time had become a leading supplier of bulbs and other products around the globe. The appliance division was then also one of the world's largest, producing refrigerators, freezers, ovens, ranges, washers, dryers, dishwashers, microwaves, disposals, compactors, air conditioners, and water purifiers. The aviation division had expanded into aircraft leasing, while other departments concentrated on electric power, medical technology, and a host of individual and commercial financial services.

Still, shareholders were not satisfied. In 1981, they shook things up by naming John F. Welch, Jr. to lead the firm. The Massachusetts native not only became the youngest person ever to head GE, but with his Ph.D. in chemical engineering he was also the first with a doctorate at the helm. Welch quickly showed that he would additionally be the first in modern times to demand big changes. Immediately, he announced that the 89-year-old institution would henceforth only compete in fields in which it could be first or second among all players.

To reach that goal, he pulled the company away from small household appliances. He downsized the workforce from 404,000 to 229,000, ending GE's longtime no-layoff policy and earning the nickname Neutron Jack (after the bomb that destroys people but leaves buildings intact). He sold $12 billion in GE businesses and purchased others worth $26 billion. Among them was the RCA Corporation and its NBC television network, although he turned right around and swapped RCA's consumer electronics division—which he deemed a loser—for a French medical technology firm. He agreed to combine GE's European interests in appliances, medical equipment, electrical distribution, and power systems with the unrelated General Electric Company of Britain. And he "delayered" every one of the company's division—going from as many as 10 or 11 management tiers in each to as few as four or five.

The combination generated some criticism even as it transformed the venerable manufacturing giant into a global service-oriented titan. It also boosted the company's market cap from $12 billion to more than $100 billion—garnering increasing admiration along with the rapidly diminishing complaints.

Above all, Jack Welch prepared GE for the 21st century by insisting that all of its businesses would consistently perform at the highest level possible. In 1995—the year he underwent triple bypass surgery and started speculation about a successor—Welch implemented his most famous effort in this regard: "Six Sigma." A quality initiative that permits just 3.4 defects per every one million possibilities, Six Sigma demands near-perfection across the board. Welch invested $200 million that first year to jump-start the program in 200 projects. When he learned it almost immediately generated $170 million in savings, it was rapidly expanded. Other firms also rushed to use it to boost their customer satisfaction, supplier quality, internal performance, and other gauges of accomplishment.

Welch's legend expanded as GE became, in 1997, the first company in the world to exceed $200 billion in market value. After teaming its NBC division with Microsoft in order to launch the groundbreaking television and Internet news service MSNBC, he aggressively expanded the list of products the company sells online—including financial services such as insurance, mutual funds, credit cards, and home mortgages. He also achieved his goal of becoming number-one or number-two in a wide array of industries—from broadcasting to appliances, aircraft engines to locomotives, medical gear to plastics. Nonetheless, he was still acquiring as many as 100 new businesses a year.

And then Welch announced that he would step down late in 2001, after 20 years on the job. At the end of 2000, GE named medical systems division boss Jeffrey R. Immelt, 44, to replace Welch. Immelt immediately became president- and chairman-elect, and began working closely with Welch until the transition was completed.

At number-five on the *Fortune* 500, with successful operations in dozens of fields and more than 100 countries, he had taken GE farther than almost anyone expected. Few were surprised, therefore, when he was offered the record book advance to explain how he did it—or with his subsequent pledge to give the entire $7.1 million and all additional earnings to charity. Welch, after all, had always been a quality guy.

soft AT&T Ford Apple McDonald's America Online FedEx CBS Philip Morris Wal-Mart Ger ic IBM Sears Roebuck Motors J.P. Morgan & Co. Union Pacific RCA Nike Intel CNN Boeing Hew ard Standard Oil Sony USX-U.S. Steel Group Agence France-Presse Levitt & Sons Walt Di ape Coca-Cola Thyssen Krupp Proctor & Gamble Yahoo! Toyota People Express Manpower Toys National Football League Kellogg Johnson Publishing Firestone Tire & Rubber Avon Products H s Ben & Jerry's Homemade REMAX Singer Sewing Shorebank Corp. Metro-Goldwyn-Mayer L.L. B einz Mic AT&T McDonald's America Online FedEx CBS Philip Morris Wal-ral Elect Sears Roebuck ors J.P. Morgan & Co. Union Pacific RCA Nike Intel CNN Bo itt-Packard dard Oil Som X-U.S. Steel Group Agence France-Presse Levitt & Sons Walt Di ape Coca-C Thysse Proctor & Gamble Yahoo! Toyota People Express Manpower Toy National Foo League logg Johnson Publishing Firestone Tire & Rubber Avon Products H s Ben & nem X Singer Sewing Shorebank Corp. Metro-Goldwyn-Mayer L.L. B einz Microsoft AT&T Ford Apple McDonald's America Online FedEx CBS Philip Morris Wal-ral Electric IBM Sears Roebuck Motors J.P. Morgan & Co. Union Pacific RCA Nike Intel CNN Bo itt-Packard Standard Oil Sony US Agence France-Presse vitt & Sons Walt Di ape Coca-Cola Thyssen Krupp P er Toy National Football League Kellogg Johnson Publishing Firesto Tire & Rubber Avon Products H s Ben & Jerry's Homemade

Number

12

IBM Corporation

Fact File:

✓ Founder: Thomas Watson Sr.
✓ Distinction: The king of technology throughout the technology age.
✓ Primary products: Computer hardware, software, peripherals, service.
✓ Annual sales: $87.548 billion.
✓ Number of employees: 307,401.
✓ Major competitors: Compaq, Hewlett-Packard, Microsoft.
✓ Chairman and CEO: Louis V. Gerstner Jr.
✓ Headquarters: Armonk, N.Y.
✓ Year founded: 1911.
✓ Web site: www.ibm.com.

Before disgruntled techno-rebels ever heard of Microsoft, IBM was the company they loved to hate. The monolithic Big Blue was the first big dog in technology, dominating the industry. (It was sued three times for antitrust violations.) From the 1920s when its tabulators, time clocks, and typewriters first set their own standards, through the 1980s when its PC became the model for desktop computing, virtually no one—technologically speaking—could escape its grasp. Factor in its infamously conformist corporate culture, and it's easy to see how International Business Machines consistently drew the ire of dissidents.

But then the company—on top since Thomas Watson Sr. peddled mechanical tabulating machines and Thomas Watson Jr. pushed early business computers—inexplicably missed several important waves in technology. It opened its PC design to everyone, but waited too long to market an operating system needed by resultant "clones." It jumped early into cyberspace, but picked the wrong vehicle in the ill-fated

Prodigy online service. It also was unprepared for a shift in corporate purchasing power, which evolved from the massive departments it had always dealt with to individuals making technology decisions in today's small companies. In 1993, its net loss hit $8 billion.

However, when Lou Gerstner took over, IBM has been remade and resurrected. Gerstner freed it from unproductive habits. He trimmed the bloated workforce, but recruited top newcomers. He introduced important products such as "hub" computers (or servers) that move data between workstations and the Internet. Most importantly, he rejected cries to disassemble the company, correctly sensing it was uniquely qualified to provide integrated solutions for an array of contemporary technological needs. Such services, rather than specific products, thus became the driving force behind his new IBM.

And it worked. Revenues hit record levels. Market capitalization grew 10-fold. Even the culture relaxed, with annual reports now featuring modern folks in blue jeans rather than automatons in dark suits. Some questioned whether it could be maintained, but Gerstner remained upbeat—targeting e-commerce as the next frontier, even as he reluctantly prepared for his retirement in the not-so-distant future.

Thomas Watson Sr. (also known as TJ) joined the company that would become IBM in 1914, the same year Thomas Watson Jr. was born. TJ left his job as second-in-command at the National Cash Register Company one year earlier. He joined the Computing-Tabulating-Recording Company as general manager, and became president after 11 months. At 40, Watson found himself with a new baby and a new business. The latter—with 1,300 employees, a half dozen North American plants, and headquarters in New York—sold everything from commercial scales to cheese slicers. Both father and son would have a lot to say about that in coming years.

TJ was an accomplished salesman, having hustled sewing machines and musical instruments before joining NCR and working his way up to general sales manager. At C-T-R he put his experience to use, paying particular attention to the Punch Card Tabulating Machine developed in 1890 for the U.S. Census Bureau. To sell it to businesses, such as railroads and insurance companies, Watson adopted numerous tactics from his previous firm. These included employing only clean-cut salesman who aggressively competed for generous performance incentives, hanging assorted inspirational slogans like "THINK" and "Make things happen" throughout the workplace, and instilling fiery company spirit by promoting employee sports teams, family outings, and even a company song.

Watson built a fanatical workforce. And within a half-dozen years tripled revenues to about $15 million before expanding into Europe, South America, Asia, and Australia. Concentrating on tabulators, time clocks and typewriters, he refocused the company and in 1924 changed its name to International Business Machines to reflect its new emphasis.

The Depression quieted most American businesses in the 1930s, but it seemed only a minor inconvenience to Watson. During the decade he unveiled new calculating machines, and gave employees medical and life insurance, a pension, and paid vacations. This kept everyone busy and loyal until the Social Security Act of 1935 was passed, bringing IBM a huge contract to maintain records for the new program's 26 million participants. To assist in what the company still calls "the biggest accounting operation of all time," Thomas Watson Jr. came aboard in 1937.

IBM was an optimistic place, but the start of World War II changed everything. TJ offered his plants to the U.S. Government, and got them producing some three dozen war-related items such as bombsights and rifles. At the same time, his son left for a five-year hitch as a B-24 pilot.

While the war raged, the line between Senior's declining reign and Junior's emergence was irrevocably drawn. In 1944 IBM completed a six-year collaboration with Harvard to develop the Mark I, or Automatic Sequence Controlled Calculator. Over 50 feet long and weighing five tons, it was the first machine capable of automatically executing long computations. Seeing few commerical possibilities, the elder Watson dismissed the new technology. But the younger Watson envisioned it as the company's future, and upon his return from the war began advocating for such development. His position ultimately won out, and in 1952 he was named IBM's president.

During the next several years the company went the way of both Watsons, moving solidly into the new age of computers while solidifying its old-world culture. A strict level of almost Victorian morality prevailed, while workers often toiled overtime and on holidays. As compensation, they were offered top benefits along with an inherent promise of lifetime employment. This created a fiercely faithful staff that eventually developed the first computer to efficiently perform basic business functions, such as billing, payroll and inventory control—thus opening new opportunities that IBM was ready and eager to address.

The younger Watson fully emerged from TJ's shadow by aggressively pursuing this new market. And in 1956—just six weeks before the elder Watson's death—Thomas Jr. was named IBM's CEO. One of his first acts was to reorganize into six autonomous divisions. He then completed the move from old-fashioned tabulators to cutting-edge computers by developing the first transistorized mainframes (which the Air Force also used to run its Ballistic Missile Early Warning System) and the first "family" of compatible business computers (which accepted interchangeable software and peripherals). He also revolutionized the way such products were sold, unbundling the hardware, software and services previously offered only as packages. The company blossomed during his tenure, which ended a year after he suffered a heart attack in 1970, growing from 72,500 to 270,000 employees and from $892 million to $8.3 billion in gross revenue. *Fortune* magazine called him "the greatest capitalist who ever lived," and he sat on the board until 1984.

Not surprisingly, life after the Watsons was not so smooth. IBM products became increasingly ingrained in everyday life, as epitomized by its supermarket checkout stations and early automatic teller machines. It remained the leader in large computers, and claimed the desktop market for itself for awhile after unveiling the PC. Old technology (like the ubiquitous Selectric typewriter) was jettisoned, and new technology (as embodied by the pioneering, but ultimately unsuccessful, Prodigy service) was embraced. But when growth peaked in 1986, a swollen, complacent workforce and corporate-wide arrogance stemming from years as the unmatched industry leader, kept IBM from pursuing potentially lucrative new directions.

By the early 1990s, IBM no longer seemed sure of its customers or the products they needed. Pressures mounted along with losses. In desperation, the board turned for the first time to an outsider—Louis V. Gerstner Jr.—and beseeched him to turn their company around.

Before Lou Gerstner, every chief executive at IBM was home-grown. Gerstner began his career with McKinsey & Co. and American Express, and then served four years as chairman and CEO of RJR Nabisco. In 1993, the year IBM posted record losses and Thomas Watson Jr. died, Gerstner moved to Big Blue despite some initial misgivings. His skeptical and outsider's perspectives would both prove critical in the years ahead.

Gerstner began with a bang, slashing annual expenses by $9 billion. Among other things this meant layoffs—unambiguously reneging on the historical promise of lifetime employment—and the newcomer had to deal with the resultant personal and cultural fallout. But that, he said later, was one vital step in getting the company back on track.

Another major reemphasis was on customer orientation, a sensibility shared by both Watsons but largely missing since their departure. This was achieved in part by revamping the product line to meet the real needs of the customer, whom Gerstner believed was mainly interested in network computing issues. He began by acquiring complementary businesses (such as Lotus Development and Tivoli Systems), and fighting pressures to split IBM into independent companies (recognizing the advantages of offering broad but integrated services).

In 1997, IBM emphatically proved its heavy-duty hardware still packed a punch. It created a machine nicknamed Deep Blue that defeated world chess champion Garry Kasparov in a six-game match. But the attention remained primarily on helping clients plan, install and operate virtually any type of high-tech network. As the century turned, a strong interest developed in e-business customers, for whom IBM could do everything—from hosting simple Web sites to orchestrating entire corporate technology programs. A reorganization early in 2000 aimed for accelerated growth in this area and also hinted at a possible successor to Gerstner, whose employment contract calls for him to remain at least until March 2002 when he turns 60. Without confirming or denying such a departure he is concentrating on building IBM's strengths in e-business, which he's targeted as his next frontier.

fric IBM Sears Roebuck Motors J.P. Morgan & Co. Union Pacific RCA Nike Intel CNN Boeing He
ard Standard Oil Sony USX-U.S. Steel Group Agence France-Presse Levitt & Sons Walt D
cape Coca-Cola Thyssen Krupp Proctor & Gamble Yahoo! Toyota People Express Manpower Toy
National Football League Kellogg Johnson Publishing Firestone Tire & Rubber Avon Products H
s Ben & Jerry's Homemade RE/MAX Singer Sewing Shorebank Corp. Metro-Goldwyn-Mayer L.L. B
Heinz Microsoft AT&T Ford Apple McDonald's America Online FedEx CBS Philip Morris Wal
ral Electric IBM Sears Roebuck Motors J.P. Morgan & Co. Union Pacific RCA Nike Intel CNN Bo
ett-Packard Standard Oil Sony USX-U.S. Steel Group Agence France-Presse Levitt & Sons Walt Di
cape Coca-Cola Thyssen Krupp Proctor & Gamble Yahoo! Toyota People Express Manpower Toy
National Football League Kellogg Johnson Publishing Firestone Tire & Rubber Avon Products H
s Ben & Jerry's Homemade RE/MAX Singer Sewing Shorebank Corp. Metro-Goldwyn-Mayer L.L. B
Heinz Microsoft AT&T Ford Apple McDonald's America Online FedEx CBS Philip Morris Wal
ral Electric IBM Sears Roebuck Motors J.P. Morgan & Co. Union Pacific RCA Nike Intel CNN Bo
ett-Packard Standard Oil Sony USX-U.S. Steel Group Agence France-Presse Levitt & Sons Walt Di
cape Coca-Cola Thyssen Krupp Proctor & Gamble Yahoo! Toyota People Express Manpower Toy
National Football League Kellogg Johnson Publishing Firestone Tire & Rubber Avon Products H
s Ben & Jerry's Homemade

Number

13

Sears, Roebuck, and Co.

Fact File:

- ✓ Founders: Richard Sears and Alvah C. Roebuck.
- ✓ Distinction: World's first mass-retailing network.
- ✓ Primary products: Apparel, home fashions, appliances, home improvement products, lawn and garden equipment.
- ✓ Annual sales: $41.071 billion.
- ✓ Number of employees: 324,000.
- ✓ Major competitors: Wal-Mart, Target, JC Penney.
- ✓ Chairman, president, and CEO: Alan J. Lacy.
- ✓ Headquarters: Hoffman Estates, Ill.
- ✓ Year founded: 1886.
- ✓ Web site: www.sears.com.

Not long ago, the arrival of a Sears catalog in any American home was an event rivaling Christmas itself. Mom paged through the thick "Wish Book" from cover to cover, carefully examining new clothes and household goods and circling those needed for the upcoming season. Dad eagerly checked out tools, and lingered over pages of auto, garden, and home improvement items. Younger kids went straight for the toys; older ones leafed through sections with fashions or sporting goods. When a must-have list was finally compiled, it was painstakingly copied onto the proper forms and slipped almost reverently into the official return envelope. After what seemed like ages, a big box (or two or three) was delivered, and the fun began anew.

In recent years, of course, the real-life equivalent of this admittedly stereotypical scene has not unfolded very often. The ever-evolving family and a hotly contested retail arena—not to mention the changes in lifestyle and technology that have both spawned and drawn from them—help see to that. But while specific goods and sales methods have shifted over the years, Sears, Roebuck and Co. remains the second-largest retailer in the world. It still reaches across vast distances to people in large cities and small towns. It still offers everything—from jewelry and shoes to fishing tackle and appliances. And it still engenders tremendous loyalty among its enormous customer base, although it must now share most of them with an increasing array of hungry competitors.

To keep up, the company has reached out to new and old shoppers alike in ways that probably would stun co-founder Richard Sears. He started things, after all, by simply peddling some gold-filled watches to coworkers along a Minnesota railroad line. Today, a mind-boggling selection of products and services is offered through some 850 mall-based stores, 1,400 specialty stores, and 650 small-town stores that mostly all bear his name. New high-tech sales tools and trendy advertising campaigns are consistently tested and deployed. And, for those who prefer to shop at home, there's even a state-of-the-art Web site designed to match competitors in the newest marketplace of all.

In the 1880s, Richard Sears was a station agent for the Minneapolis and St. Louis railway in North Redwood, Minn. To fill the quiet days and pick up extra cash, he sold lumber and coal to residents of the area. When a neighboring jeweler received a shipment of watches that he didn't want, Sears offered to take them off his hands. He sold them for a profit to other station agents, and realized that there was money to be made in this market. In 1886 he formed the R.W. Sears Watch Company in Minneapolis and set off upon a new career in retailing.

Success came quickly and the ambitious Sears began looking for ways to expand. During the very next year he relocated to Chicago. Immediately upon his arrival, he sought help in his new venture through a classified ad in the *Chicago Daily News*. One of the respondents was Alvah C. Roebuck, an experienced watchmaker from Indiana. Sears hired him on the spot. The two men, both in their 20s, kicked off a business partnership that would permanently alter America's retailing landscape.

In 1893, they changed their corporate name to Sears, Roebuck and Co. At the time, about two-thirds of the nation's 60 million residents were living in rural areas and most of them—farmers in particular—were forced to purchase all of their goods from small, high-priced general stores. Sears and Roebuck were among several entrepreneurs who felt they could offer better deals through mail-order catalogs. Others who hit upon the same strategy included fellow Chicago merchant Aaron Montgomery Ward, who already had turned it into a multimillion-dollar enterprise. By purchasing products in bulk and utilizing the railroads and a growing package delivery system, these companies became rising commercial stars.

Richard Sears knew the rural market from his days in Minnesota. He also knew how to write catalog copy that convinced people to purchase what he was selling. By 1893 the company's sales hit $400,000. Two years later, Sears and his partner were churning out catalogs with more than 500 pages featuring watches and jewelry as well as shoes, women's clothing, wagons, fishing gear, stoves, furniture, dishes and glassware, musical instruments, saddles, firearms, buggies, bicycles, and baby carriages. Sales jumped to $750,000 and Chicago clothing manufacturer Julius Rosenwald was brought aboard to help organize the booming business.

The company moved into larger quarters and began construction on a 40-acre, $5 million plant and office building on Chicago's West Side. Roebuck, who was in ill health, resigned soon after. Rosenwald became vice president, and in 1901 was additionally named treasurer. Five years later Sears and Rosenwald decided to take the company public to obtain additional capital. Its stock symbol, still a lone "S," underscores the pioneering place that it holds in America's business and financial marketplace.

That same year, the company moved into its new headquarters and opened an office in Dallas to serve the growing southwestern U.S. market. Sears hoped to ultimately open 10 such regional facilities. His rapidly expanding business was experiencing some growing pains, however, primarily related to shipping snafus. To solve them, company officials designed and implemented an elaborate system that helped efficiently handle an even greater sales volume. According to company lore, Henry Ford was among those who traveled to the plant to study these advanced assembly-line techniques.

The catalog was fine-tuned during the early days of the 20th century, but it still carried an astounding assortment of products at prices that seem incredible today. Men's suits were $9.95, while a "Stradivarius model violin" went for just $6.10. To help distribute even more catalogs, Sears hit upon an innovative marketing scheme: He asked customers to pass them out to friends and neighbors, and offered premiums (such as bicycles or sewing machines) when these secondary recipients placed orders. After experimenting with this plan in Iowa, Sears rolled it out nationally.

Despite all this, significant changes in American life began threatening mail-order sales. The growth of cities and their steadily improving modes of transportation, meant less captive rural customers who relied upon the Wish Book. A proliferation of chain stores that sprang up around the country to meet this new reality simultaneously created a major new form of competition. Sears decided to fight back by opening its own stores in various cities. Robert E. Wood—a company vice president who later became president and board chairman—was placed in charge of the effort.

The first store opened in Sears's Chicago plant in 1925. It was a huge success, and seven more immediately followed. Within two years, 27 stores were operating. By 1929, the company had 319. Thousands of customers flocked to them, and retail sales topped mail order for the first time in 1931. "Leases can't be signed fast enough, stores can't be readied fast enough, personnel can't be hired fast enough," one company official noted. This popularity helped convince Sears to begin offering products under brand names of its own. The unveiling of Craftsman, Kenmore, and DieHard items came next.

Sears decided to move into other areas as well. It created Allstate Insurance as a wholly-owned subsidiary in 1931. In later years, it added the Dean Witter Reynolds financial organization, Coldwell Banker real estate company, and Discover credit card business to complete what it saw as a collection of full-line customer services. Catalog sales offices were launched in towns too small to support a full-scale retail outlet, while stores were also opened outside the United States (Cuba was the first locale in 1942, followed by Mexico, South America, Europe, and Canada.) The continual growth demanded additional management space, and in 1969 construction was begun on a new headquarters building in downtown Chicago. When completed four years later, the 110-story Sears Tower became the world's tallest building.

The world itself kept changing, however, and even a company ranked number 15 in the *Fortune* 500 was forced to continually adapt. Several reorganizations were initiated in the 1980s and 90s. Underperforming stores were closed while a Sears Merchandise Group was formed to oversee core businesses such as apparel, housewares, and automotive products. Dean Witter and Allstate were spun off into separate companies and Coldwell Banker was sold. Credit policies were tightened to reduce delinquencies. Corporate headquarters was relocated to a 200-acre campus west of Chicago's O'Hare International Airport. The vaunted catalog even mutated into the Sears Shop-at-Home Service, which now features several smaller specialty books along with home repair and improvement operations.

Under Arthur C. Martinez, who retired as chairman and CEO at the end of 2000 and was replaced by long-time Sears executive Alan J. Lacy, these adaptations and innovations continued. A major image makeover began with the widely lauded advertising campaign emphasizing "the softer side of Sears" and subsequent efforts stressing low prices that match competitors. Advanced merchandising tools—including a high-tech chain-wide computer system—have thrust the company into the 21st century. Weak product lines are being eliminated. And a $100 million push to tout its emergence in cyberspace is an effort to pull younger customers through its doors.

All this does not mean officials are ignoring the company's storied past in a single-minded attempt to move into the future. An early TV commercial for its Web site featured a family from the 1950s looking at new appliances through an old-fashioned Sears department store window. And a section mimicking the old Wish Book is a big part of the online effort.

14

General Motors Corp.

Fact File:

- ✓ Founder: William C. Durant.
- ✓ Distinction: World's number-one automaker, and largest company in terms of sales.
- ✓ Primary products: Cars, trucks and related parts.
- ✓ Annual sales: $176.558 billion.
- ✓ Number of employees: 388,000.
- ✓ Major competitors: DaimlerChrysler, Ford, Toyota.
- ✓ Chairman: John F. Smith Jr.; President and CEO: G. Richard Wagoner Jr.
- ✓ Headquarters: Detroit, Mich.
- ✓ Year founded: 1908.
- ✓ Web site: www.gm.com.

O n the surface, it would seem that G. Richard Wagoner Jr. and Alfred P. Sloan have little in common. Sloan, the long-time leader at automotive giant General Motors, began his storied reign in 1923 when both industry and product were relatively new, competitors numbered in the dozens, and management had undergone a major upheaval. Wagoner, the most recent to assume control at GM, took over in June 2000 when both industry and product were quite mature, competitors were few and rapidly dwindling, and management had been stable for nearly a decade.

Nonetheless, Wagoner shares more with his legendary predecessor than the fact that he is the youngest person since Sloan to lead the world's largest automaker. Both, after all, took over a sprawling company that sported an impressive pedigree along with an immediate need for a good swift kick in the transmission. And both found themselves facing a confluence of surprisingly similar problems—ongoing corporate arrogance and an archaic administrate approach that was regularly unable to meet the ever-changing needs of its constituents and times, chief among them.

The ascension of Wagoner to GM's top spot may have been unusually smooth for this often tumultuous operation, but it will undoubtedly prove no less critical than Sloan's momentous tenure as the firm prepares for its future. For while the company's extensive product lines and vast global reach and impressive statistical data remain quite formidable (taken together, they make it the world's largest corporation in terms of sales) without the innovation and drive that marked Sloan's 33-year term in office they simply may not be enough to help Wagoner move it successfully from the 20th century into the 21st.

General Motors was the brainchild of William Crapo Durant, a brilliant salesman who was born in Boston in 1861. After his father's foray into the stock market ended badly, Durant's mother moved the family to the upper Midwest. There, her own father had made a fortune in the lumber business before serving as the mayor of Flint and the governor of Michigan. And there, Bill Durant also found his calling.

High school held little appeal for the ambitious youngster, and Durant dropped out long before graduation. He immediately took a job as a salesman for a local cigar manufacturer, and proved a natural in the field by selling 22,000 cigars on his very first sales trip. In 1885, he took a spin in a friend's wagon and the particularly smooth ride changed his life—convincing him, then and there, that better business opportunities lay in the fledgling field of transportation. Durant offered the manufacturer $1,500 for patent rights to his unique suspension system, and he hooked up with a partner. By 1900, he had built the Durant-Dort carriage company into America's largest.

Durant quickly grew rich but bored. So, when he was able to drive an early horseless carriage around Flint, he knew it held the key to his future. In 1904 he purchased the Buick Motor Company, which was turning out decent vehicles but was in constant financial trouble. His sales savvy immediately translated into orders for some 1,100 cars, which was more than 25-times the total that Buick had produced during its entire three-year history. To meet this demand, Durant sold stock in the firm to everyone he knew. In 1905, he had Buick building 725 vehicles a year. By 1908, annual production hit 8,820 and it became the number-one car manufacturer in the United States, outselling numbers two and three combined.

Durant, however, felt that bigger would be better—even in a business that was dependent upon the fickle tastes of the public. So, on September 16, 1908, he formed the General Motors Corporation to bring numerous auto types and styles together under one roof. His new venture absorbed Buick, and then bought Olds Motor Vehicle, Cadillac Automobile, and some 20 smaller firms including Ewing, Marquette, and Elmore. Durant also believed that producing his own parts would be more efficient and save money, so he expanded vertically as well and bought companies that could supply his manufacturers with glass, paint, sheet metal and other critical components.

In its first year, GM sold an astonishing 25,000 cars and trucks and reported net sales of $29 million. But many of Durant's deals were ill-conceived and he soon proved far more adept at building a business than operating one. Within two years, GM was in serious financial trouble. Durant had to turn to a syndicate of bankers for a loan to save it from ruin. One of the loan's conditions barred him from the company for five years, but Durant could not sit still. While the bankers were righting General Motors with a more conservative approach, he founded the Chevrolet Motor Company and quickly made it a huge success. By 1915—the year his banishment from GM was to end—Durant had built Chevy into the country's biggest car maker.

He was itching to get back to his baby, though, and began buying up shares of GM stock. In 1918, he regained control and brought Chevrolet—along with other properties such as the Hyatt Roller Bearing Company—into its fold. He began expanding once more, too, enlarging existing plants, starting construction on a new research laboratory as well as a 15-story Detroit headquarters, and acquiring more companies, such as Fisher Body. He also moved GM into the finance business by creating the General Motors Acceptance Corporation in 1919, the same year GM made more than $60 million in profits on sales of nearly 400,000 cars and trucks. Once more, Durant's big plans resulted in big-time fiscal disaster. GM's stock price tumbled from $42 to $14 in just seven months, and Durant was financially destroyed. Bankers were again summoned to bail out the company, and in 1920 he was again forced to resign.

One good thing that came out of this was the appointment of Alfred Sloan as executive vice president. Sloan, a Hyatt manager joined GM after its acquisition. He instantly set about implementing a revolutionary administrative system that essentially called for centralized management and budget control, decision-making by committee, and the delegation of day-to-day responsibilities to appropriate divisions. He also separated the various automotive operations so that each would create specific cars for specific consumers, who then would move from one to another. Chevrolet became the car for the masses; Cadillac, the standard-bearer among luxury vehicles; Oldsmobile and Buick built their own distinct audiences; and Oakland, which later was renamed Pontiac, found its niche as a performance machine.

In 1923, Sloan was named GM's president. Eight years later, the company began its uninterrupted reign as the world's leader in car and truck sales. Sloan retained his top spot in the company until 1956; he then became honorary chairman until his death in 1966 at age 91.

General Motors flourished as the automobile became ingrained in society. Its total vehicle sales hit 25 million in 1940. However, World War II hit, and GM's factories were refit to support the U.S. effort. More than $12.3 billion worth of airplane parts, trucks, tanks, guns, shells, and other items rolled out of GM plants during the following years. When regular production resumed in 1946, new automakers like Packard, Studebaker and Nash joined the fray. Most, though, didn't last very long.

Aided by technical innovations like power steering and power brakes, along with design advances (that led, among other things, to the introduction of the Corvette) GM recorded its first billion-dollar profit in the 1950s. A decade later it had produced over 100 million vehicles. The company was also still atop the automotive pack in the 1970s, although Japanese competitors Toyota and Nissan had climbed to numbers two and three. When these companies passed U.S. firms in total production for the first time in 1980, General Motors struck back by linking up. It signed an agreement to jointly make Toyotas in California, invested heavily in Isuzu, and arranged for Suzuki to produce small cars for sale in America.

Still, during the 1980s, GM's market share dropped from 44 percent to 35 percent. It remained the world's largest motor vehicle manufacturer, with 700,000 employees in 149 U.S. plants, 13 Canadian facilities, and operations in 29 other countries. But the writing was on the wall, and the tradition-bound management team did not know how to respond. Although some of their ideas held promise—such as the Saturn line, and an electric vehicle called the Impact—factory inefficiencies began taking their toll, vehicle designs grew unimaginative, product quality declined, and consumers turned away in drives.

GM was forced to close plants in order to maintain a profitable edge. This was a PR disaster, and one Michael Moor poignantly exploited in his 1989 film *Roger & Me* (1989). The clever documentary followed Moore's attempt to track down GM chairman Roger Smith and hold him accountable for the company's actions. Called a "revenge comedy" by noted critic Roger Ebert (who gave it four stars), the movie helped GM's reputation decline...along with its sales.

GM sales remained far ahead of its nearest rivals, but the company suffered multibillion dollar losses in 1990 and 1991. Its board rebelled by dumping the chairman, president, vice chairman and executive vice president. Jack Smith was picked to fill the top posts. By 1995, he had begun turning things around. That year, GM reported its highest-ever net income.

A costly 1998 strike and continued assault from foreign competitors knocked GM's U.S. market share down to 27.7 percent—the lowest it had been since Sloan's arrival. Smith voluntarily stepped into the board suite to make way for Wagoner, a well-regarded up-and-comer who had filled a variety of roles at GM during 23 of his 47 years. Wagoner's mission was immediately made clear: Continue cutting costs and upgrading vehicle designs for today's consumers, and do it fast.

Can he succeed, and make this industrial-age behemoth a winner in the lean-and-mean technology era? History may be with him, but only time will tell.

15

J.P. Morgan & Company

Fact File:

✓ Founder: J. Pierpont Morgan.
✓ Distinction: Preserved and expanded the American financial system.
✓ Primary products: Commercial banking and investment services.
✓ Annual sales: $18.110 billion.
✓ Number of employees: 15,512.
✓ Major competitors: Deutsche Bank, Goldman Sachs, Merrill Lynch.
✓ Chairman and CEO: Douglas A. "Sandy" Warner III.
✓ Headquarters: New York, N.Y.
✓ Year founded: 1854.
✓ Web site: www.jpmorgan.com.

The fabled House of Morgan first surfaced as a financial powerhouse in the mid-19th century. It was instrumental in the formation of corporate icons such as U.S. Steel and General Electric. At one time, it controlled a significant portion of America's railroads. It loaned millions to the governments of France, England, Mexico, and Russia. It helped preserve America's monetary system more than once when it was threatened with collapse. It endured the Great Depression, two World Wars, and federal regulations that forced it to shed one of its most lucrative businesses. Despite being such a major player in the business world, however, it could not survive the massive changes that transformed its industry in recent years.

With roots going back to a London merchant bank opened in the 1830s, J.P. Morgan & Company has long been more than a run-of-the-mill financial institution.

From its headquarters on Wall Street and offices in some three dozen countries, the firm assembled by three generations of Morgans has served as fiscal advisor to the most prominent and powerful people on earth. It has underwritten some of the largest stock offerings and corporate mergers ever initiated. It was once the primary source of U.S. Government financing, and members of the family from which it takes its name are widely considered the most influential financiers of modern times.

But that doesn't mean the Morgans were always held in high esteem. With equal parts greed and guile, they often made bold moves to advance their interests at the expense of others. They flaunted their successes in public—at times when many Americans were struggling to get by. They had a none-too-subtle fondness for beautiful women, expensive cigars, immense yachts, and world-class art. They acted as if America's economic landscape was their own private playground, ultimately alienating the government they often assisted as well as many people they made rich.

The firm's attitude and approach shifted markedly over the last 50 years, but changes in the financial marketplace eventually caught up. And in the fall of 2000, Morgan announced its acquisition by another storied name in the world of banking—one whose roots, if not its influence and importance, go even deeper than its own.

In 1838, American businessman George Peabody opened a merchant bank in London. A few years later he took on a partner named Junius Spencer Morgan, the descendent of a prominent New England trading family who took over the firm in 1854 and renamed it J.S. Morgan & Company. Morgan then ran the operation for more than three decades, serving as a key financial connection between Britain and the U.S. and setting the tone for its future by loaning $50 million to France during the Franco-Prussian War.

Before leaving for Europe, Morgan had a son. After attending schools in Boston, Switzerland, and Germany, the young J. Pierpont Morgan returned to New York for a job as an accountant with a firm representing his father's company. During the 1860s and 1870s he worked for several investment concerns, including Drexel, Harjes & Company of Paris. He inherited his father's business after the senior Morgan's death in 1890, changing the official name to J.P. Morgan & Company and consolidating its European and American interests. He also made his first mark on the financial world just a few years later, assembling a bond issue to resupply the U.S. Government's depleted gold reserves and relieve a treasury crisis.

With the company based back in New York, J. Pierpont started turning it into a prime developer of American business. He began with a foray into the railway industry, arranging a rate agreement between two of the largest competitors—the New York Central and Pennsylvania railroads—and then helping reorganize others including the Southern, Erie, and Northern Pacific. As partial compensation he accepted stock in the companies and positions on their boards of directors, greatly

</

Number

20

Cable News Network

Fact File:

✓ Founder: Ted Turner.
✓ Distinction: World's first live, round-the-clock,
  all-news television network.
✓ Primary products: TV, radio, and Internet news programs.
✓ Annual sales: Unavailable.
✓ Number of employees: 4,000.
✓ Major competitors: CNBC, MSNBC, Fox News Channel.
✓ Chairman, President and CEO: W. Thomas Johnson.
✓ Headquarters: Atlanta, Ga.
✓ Year founded: 1980.
✓ Web site: www.cnn.com.

Many Americans tuned into Cable News Network for the very first time when former Beatle John Lennon was gunned down in New York, exactly six months after the station's 1980 debut. Stunned fans—at least those in the 1.7 million homes then capable of receiving the all-news channel—found they could get updates on the riveting story whenever they wanted. For those accustomed to obtaining news on TV only when the major networks and their affiliates decided to broadcast it, this proved to be both exhilarating and addictive.

It was not yet enough, though, to put the fledgling station on the map. Unknown on-air personalities at its Atlanta headquarters and eight bureaus across the United States struggled to gain respectability. Expenses were so tight that ceiling panels sometimes crashed down during live reports. Bargain-basement electronic equipment regularly failed. Few viewers even knew of its existence.

But all that changed as CNN improved its resources and a series of compelling events drove an audience to its spot on the cable dial. As U.S. hostages were released by their Iranian captors, as an Air Florida jet slid into Washington's icy Potomac, and as the Challenger space shuttle exploded over Florida, more Americans accessed CNN and many found it a credible source for 24-hour coverage of the stories that had their neighbors talking. By the time 18-month-old Baby Jessica tumbled into a Texas well in 1987 and captivated the nation for 58 hours until her successful rescue, CNN was the place to turn for breaking news. Four years later, when Operation Desert Storm mobilized and American F-117s began strafing Baghdad, some 11.5 million viewers were glued to its coverage from the besieged Iraqi capital and surrounding flash points.

Today, of course, CNN is one of the world's most respected outlets for television news. Specialized auxiliary channels focus exclusively on headlines, finance and sports; others broadcast in languages including Spanish and Turkish. Radio stations and an array of Web sites have been added. Some 78 million U.S. households, and more than a billion people worldwide, have access to at least one of its services. And now, as its corporate parent is absorbed by the world's largest Internet company and aggressive competitors are just a few remote-control clicks away, it prepares to do battle in the new millenium.

CNN first went on-air on June 1, 1980, the result of a fusion of new technologies and the vision of a little-known entrepreneur named Ted Turner. Before its debut, producers at the dominant Big Three networks in New York determined when Americans would get their news. With the advent of CNN, viewers could make that choice themselves at any hour of the day.

Turner (whose given name is Robert Edward Turner III) was born in Cincinnati in 1938. At age 9, his family moved to Georgia, where Robert Edward Turner II owned a business specializing in billboard ads. After graduating from Brown University—where he was vice president of the debating union and commodore of the university yacht club—young Ted took a job with the family firm as an account executive. In 1960, he became general manager of one of Turner Advertising Company's branch offices. Three years later, business troubles drove his father to commit suicide and Turner assumed control of the ailing venture. As president and chief operating officer for the next 33 years, he slowly restored it to profitability.

Inspired by his success, Turner branched out by purchasing Atlanta's Channel 17 in 1970. Within three years, he transformed the struggling UHF outlet into one of the country's few profitable independent stations. But Turner still was not satisfied. When he discovered communication satellites he instinctively knew that they would change the lives of TV viewers everywhere. He renamed his station WTBS, for Turner Broadcasting System, and on December 17, 1976, became one of the first to use this new technology to broadcast a "superstation" to the coast-to-coast cable audience now available and hungry for content. That same year he bought the

Atlanta Braves baseball team to grab additional mass-appeal programming for the station. In 1977, while he was also achieving national recognition for piloting his yacht Courageous to victory in the America's Cup, he purchased the Atlanta Hawks basketball team for the same purpose.

The novel approach boosted Turner's TV revenues beyond his wildest dreams, and whetted his appetite for even more cable outlets. Struck by the lack of national news available, Turner created CNN in 1980. Two years later he launched a companion service dubbed Headline News to offer nothing but the day's major stories every half hour. In 1985, he went global with CNN International.

As cable television was methodically made available in practically every corner of the United States, Turner's various channels began building an audience. But numerous technical glitches, an initially unknown cast of on-air personalities, and undisguised skepticism from traditional broadcast news outlets kept them from attaining widespread acceptance at the start. That all changed, though, as equipment improved and accidents faded, newscasters established followings, and Turner's ventures consistently turned bad news into compelling TV. Lennon's assassination in 1980, the Iranian hostage release in 1981, and the Air Florida jet mishap in 1982 were merely the first national touchstones that his 24-hour news sources fed to a waiting public. By the time of the 1986 Challenger explosion and 1987 Baby Jessica rescue, CNN had all the resources ready to competently provide constant live images and a feeling of connection to the growing nationwide audience bent on following the dramas. When tanks rolled across Tiananmen Square in 1989 and scud missiles streaked across the Baghdad sky in 1991, viewership had become worldwide.

But Turner, now well known as a deal-maker and risk-taker, did not stand still. A year after founding the Goodwill Games in 1985 as an alternative to the Olympics, he purchased the MGM/UA Entertainment Company's highly regarded library of more than 4,000 films and television shows—and once again provided his various stations with exclusive programming that they could air without licensing fees. Turner incurred the wrath of Hollywood by "colorizing" many of the classic black-and-white films obtained in the latter deal, and the debt he sustained from both purchases forced him to sell several assets. Nonetheless, he continued expanding with the launch of Turner Network Television (or TNT) in 1988 and the Cartoon Network in 1992, both of which also relied extensively on the movies and shows he picked up in earlier transactions. Then, in 1996, Turner hit the jackpot and sold everything to Time Warner Inc. for $7.5 billion. His former holdings now a subsidiary of the world's largest media and entertainment conglomerate, Turner became vice-chairman (and largest shareholder) of the combined company and head of its cable networks.

All has not been completely smooth sailing for Turner and his operations, of course. There have been troubling excesses as CNN and its sister stations tried to meet the demands of a diverse audience, with criticism often leveled during its tabloid-like coverage of the O.J. Simpson trial, Clinton impeachment drama, and Elian Gonzales saga. And what many believe to be the lowest point came in 1998 when CNN's NewsStand show incorrectly reported that U.S. forces used nerve gas on American defectors in Laos during the 1970s. (CNN later retracted the story and fired several staffers, while Turner called the incident a terrible embarrassment to him and the network.) But, each time, the stations managed to fully rebound, and their status as reliable news sources reached what was probably an all-time high as the new millenium began.

CNN celebrated its 20th anniversary in Atlanta on June 1, 2000, with fireworks and video clips of its top moments. It was preparing to move under new ownership, too, as just before the calendar turned and Time Warner had announced that it was merging with America Online. Turner would become vice chairman of the new AOL Time Warner, overseeing its combined cable networks division with all the old Turner properties, along with Home Box Office (HBO), Cinemax, the Warner Bros. International Networks, and Time Warner's interests in Comedy Central and Court TV. He would no longer have direct control of these entities, however, and was said to be angered by that.

In another good-news-bad-news paradox, the big bash was held as CNN recorded its lowest monthly ratings in nine years—a fact generally attributed to new cable competitors, primarily CNBC, MSNBC, and the Fox News Channel, which were luring away significant portions of its once exclusive audience. In an attempt to boost those numbers and reduce its reliance on major one-time events, officials began developing more regularly scheduled programs, documentaries, and specials. They were also hoping that AOL and its 22 million subscribers could help bring CNN back to news domination.

Still, there was a lot to celebrate. CNN remains the world's number-one news network, with nine of the 10 highest-rated news programs on U.S. basic cable and more than 6.7 billion annual page impressions dispersed among its various Web sites. It has the world's most widely syndicated television newsfeed, and a network of more than 600 affiliates in the United States and Canada and 800 worldwide. Along with its original three channels, associated businesses now include CNNfn (launched in 1995 to cover financial developments), CNN/Sports Illustrated (an all-sports channel that debuted in 1996), CNN en Español (Spanish-language programming with 8 million subscribers), CNN Airport Network (offering traveler-oriented broadcasts in 27 U.S. airports), CNNRadio, and more.

And, without fear of contradiction, it can forever lay claim to singlehandedly changing the landscape of television news.

The Boeing Company

Fact File:

✓ Founder: William E. Boeing.
✓ Distinction: Evolved with aviation industry from biplanes to Lunar Orbiters.
✓ Primary products: Commercial and military aircrafts, rockets, satellites.
✓ Annual sales: $57.993 billion.
✓ Number of employees: 197,000.
✓ Major competitors: Airbus Industries, EADS, Lockheed Martin.
✓ Chairman and CEO: Philip M. Condit; president and COO: Harry C. Stonecipher.
✓ Headquarters: Seattle, Wash.
✓ Year founded: 1916.
✓ Web site: www.boeing.com.

For as long as there has been an aviation business, the Boeing name has been part of it. Just a few years after the Wright brothers made their first flight at Kitty Hawk, William Boeing attended the first American air show in Los Angeles. He immediately saw the possibilities, and over the next several years explored various facets of the exciting new industry. He rode a biplane from atop a wing, took flying lessons from an early barnstormer, and spearheaded the design of a seaplane. But when he bought an old Seattle shipyard to open an airplane manufacturing operation in 1916, his involvement became official.

Over the next eight-and-a-half decades, his Boeing Company weathered an ebb and flow that spelled the end to most of its once-mighty competitors. It did so by snagging virtually every opportunity that surfaced—from the first U.S. mail air routes, to massive military contracts, to domination of commercial aviation, to a major role in the space program. It has long been the top producer of commercial jets, and with various acquisitions also became the largest aerospace company in the world.

While cyclical downturns over the years devastated one aircraft or aerospace firm after another, Boeing battled back effectively with imagination and diversification. For example, it began United Airlines and employed the first female flight attendant and as an early global enterprise developed customers in 145 countries. Its vast litany of innovations includes aviation icons such as the B-52 bomber and 737 passenger plane (the best-selling jetliner in aviation history), along with the Lunar Orbiter and Saturn V booster (launcher of Apollo spacecraft on their journeys to the moon).

But none of the challenges Boeing has encountered provides immunity from those it faces today. In fact, with the 21st century barely underway, a European rival unveiled a superjumbo jet that siphoned attention—and sales—from Boeing's existing alternative. Trade magazines and Seattle-area newspapers speculated that without extraordinary effort, Boeing might soon find itself the world's number-two plane maker. Not surprisingly, Boeing prepared once again to fight back.

The Wright brothers made their historic first flight in 1903, the same year Detroit native William Boeing left Yale Engineering College to seek his fortune in the Pacific Northwest. The timber industry was red hot, and the 22-year-old quickly struck it rich in the lush forests outside Grays Harbor, Wash. After moving to Seattle, he heard about an air show in Los Angeles. Boeing attended and fell in love with what he saw, and upon his return began engaging a Navy engineer named George Conrad Westervelt in endless conversations about the future of flight.

Westervelt had taken aeronautics courses at MIT, and shared Boeing's infatuation with air travel. The two flew on an early biplane—the type requiring both pilot and passenger to sit on one wing—and pondered variations at Seattle's University Club. Before Boeing left for California in August 1915 to take flying lessons, he asked his friend to design a more practical craft. Construction on the resultant twin-float seaplane, dubbed B&W for the pair's last names, began soon after his return.

Boeing built a combination hangar-boathouse beside Lake Union. During the first half of 1916 began construction on two B&W seaplanes. The Navy sent Westervelt east before they were done, so Boeing finished on his own. On June 15, he took the plane nicknamed "Bluebill" on its maiden flight when the scheduled pilot didn't arrive on time. Exactly one month later, he incorporated his airplane manufacturing business as the Pacific Aero Products Company. He bought 998 of the 1,000 shares and moved operations to the former Health's shipyard on the Duwamish River. A year later, he changed the name of his business to Boeing Airplane Company.

Bursting with optimism over his new enterprise, Boeing assembled a 28-person staff of pilots, carpenters, seamstresses and other specialized workers. The B&W didn't sell, but World War I was underway and for the first time the United States was using airplanes in battle. Boeing knew the Navy would need planes for training, and believed his Model C filled the bill. Navy officials agreed following a Florida test flight, and ordered 50. Boeing expanded his payroll to 337 to build them, but—in a pattern that would become uncomfortably common in the years ahead—saw the order cut in half as the war drew to a close. To keep afloat, he had workers switch to building furnishings for local shops as well as a type of flat-bottomed boat called a sea sled.

Boeing wasn't through with planes, though. In 1919 he and a pilot flew 60 letters from British Columbia to Seattle, marking the first international air mail delivery into the United States. He built many new commercial aircraft models over the next few years, including the first to fly over Mount Ranier. The Army Air Service also placed a few healthy orders for fighter biplanes, but Boeing knew that he had to come up with a solid plan for producing and selling a steady number of products to a wide variety of customers if he hoped to survive. To that end he bought the Stearman Aircraft Company in Kansas, and opened Boeing Aircraft of Canada and the Boeing School of Aeronautics in California. And in 1927—the same year Charles Lindbergh made the first solo nonstop flight from New York to Paris—Boeing contracted with the U.S. Postal Department to run the coveted airmail route from Chicago to San Francisco.

At last, Boeing could efficiently use his planes while promoting them to others. To operate a route that could effectively carry passengers along with the mail, he founded Boeing Air Transport, the predecessor to United Airlines. Bowing to Prohibition, his wife Bertha inaugurated the first flight with orange-flavored soda water. During the following year, nearly a million pounds of mail and express packages, and almost 1,900 passengers, took the 22-and-one-half-hour trip. This helped kick start the idea of passenger air travel and incite a demand that—in conjunction with military orders and, later, space-related products—would keep Boeing on top for decades.

Much changed during ensuing years, but Boeing's continually broadening lineup consistently dominated its fields. His companies built airplanes and parts, including engines and propellers. They delivered mail. They maintained airports. They ran airlines. When single-winged planes replaced biplanes, Boeing's were first out of the hangar. His Yankee Clipper inaugurated regular airmail service across the Atlantic. His luxurious Stratoliner was remade as the military C-75 after the bombing of Pearl Harbor. The next was the B-29, which dropped atomic bombs on Hiroshima and Nagasaki. Government cancellations after the war again led to massive layoffs, but this time orders for long-range civilian planes replaced them, and the company pressed on. The development of jets and a continuing demand from the defense department often kept the company going full tilt. By the time William Boeing died in 1956, his aircrafts were capable of circling the globe. And, for the first time, airlines were carrying more non-commuting passengers than trains.

The 1960s put America, and Boeing, on a new path. President Kennedy promised a man on the moon, and the company loaned the government 2,000 executives to help make it happen. Its Lunar Orbiter scouted possible landing areas and its

Lunar Roving Vehicle explored the ground. Its Saturn V first-stage booster launched the Apollo craft into space.

Boeing 707s were utilized for years to transport government officials. The plane that carried the president would use the call sign "Air Force One." In 1962, two 707s were adapted specifically for use by the president and were officially given the permanent call sign Air Force One. These models served as the presidential aircraft until 1990, when they were replaced by two new Boeing 747s.

But while it continued building more advanced airplanes, such as the 490-passenger transatlantic 747 jumbo jet, Boeing also kept hitting employment peaks and valleys. Nearly 50,000 workers were dismissed in 1970 when the United States abruptly ended its supersonic transport program. Boeing responded by diversifying yet again, this time setting up a computer services company, an irrigation project in eastern Oregon, and a desalinization plant in the Virgin Islands. It also built three huge wind turbines along the Columbia River, constructed voice scramblers for police departments, and manufactured light-rail cars for several municipalities. Obviously, the more things changed the more they stayed the same.

But Boeing has remained primarily focused on commerical aircrafts, military hardware, and various utilities related to space. Its leaders have reiterated the company's long-term commitment to lead in all operational areas, absorbing top competitors Rockwell International in 1996, McDonnell Douglas in 1997, and the Hughes Electronics communications satellite business in early 2000. An unprecedented 40-day strike by engineers and technicians a few months later, however, badly impacted commerical and military production. It also trimmed the company's value by $5.3 billion.

The walkout left some bitterness on both sides, but the company and its employees plunged ahead once more when it ended. Just a few weeks after the strike, Boeing announced a new way for passengers to surf the Net and check e-mail from their laptops during flight. Shortly after, though, it was shaken once again by the announcement that its arch-rival Airbus Industries had outsold it for the first time in new aircraft orders. Further, a new Airbus superjumbo jet was attracting attention and sales that previously went to Boeing's biggest transatlantic models.

In typical Boeing fashion, the company quickly trumpeted its answer: the massive 747x Stretch. It hardly mattered that the Stretch didn't yet exist; Boeing had pulled off much more difficult transformations in the century since its founder discovered commercial aviation.

Hewlett-Packard Co.

Fact File:

✓ Founders: Bill Hewlett and David Packard.
✓ Distinction: Leader in technology, and the business world that produces it.
✓ Primary products: Computers, printing and imaging products, related services.
✓ Annual sales: $42.370 billion.
✓ Number of employees: 84,400.
✓ Major competitors: Compaq, IBM, Xerox.
✓ Chairman, CEO and President: Carleton S. "Carly" Fiorina.
✓ Headquarters: Palo Alto, Calif.
✓ Year founded: 1939.
✓ Web site: www.hp.com.

As the 21st century approached, the Hewlett-Packard Company faced a significant dilemma. Justifiably acknowledged as Silicon Valley's original startup, it literally began in a garage and unequivocally grew into one of the world's top computer companies. Ever since its audio oscillator was picked up by Walt Disney Studios in 1939 for use in the original *Fantasia*, HP had consistently produced state-of-the-art electronic gear that was the envy of its industry. From that first product through calculators, computers, printers and imaging peripherals, Hewlett-Packard was always one to watch.

In addition, the company was always a great place to work. Its founders pioneered the concept of Management By Walking Around, which encouraged leaders to stay in close touch with their employees. It eschewed time clocks and offered flexible work schedules. It was one of the first large American firms to decentralize its operations and empower its workers. It provided a superior salary-and-benefits package. It even institutionalized these and other components of its vaunted corporate culture through adoption of The HP Way, an official document that stresses trust and openness. About the only criticism ever leveled at HP, in fact, concerned the historical lack of women in the ranks of its upper management.

As the company prepared to usher in the new century, however, all this was no longer adequate. Its once-experimental corporate structure was proving an ill fit for the networked age. Quaint habits—like an odd 87-hour pay period that was implemented decades ago for a type of worker HP no longer employs—were causing unnecessary headaches. Innovations in software and other key areas often went unnoticed by the public (as well as by many members of the all-important investment community). Competitors were surging. Internet activity was lagging.

And so, in mid-1999, Hewlett-Packard broke the mold once more by naming Carleton S. "Carly" Fiorina as its president and CEO. The first woman ever to lead one of the companies that comprise the Dow Jones Industrial average—and the first outsider ever to lead HP—the 45-year-old veteran of AT&T spinoff, Lucent, immediately embarked on a massive corporate overhaul. "We decided to transform this company," she explained. Fiorina's subsequent actions certainly stunned some tradition-bound observers. Others—including many employees, customers, and investors—were more positively impressed.

A half-century before garage-based technology startups on the West Coast became a cliché, a pair of 26-year-old electrical engineers was working on electronic products in their own one-car shed in northern California. Bill Hewlett and David Packard had just $538 (along with a string of disappointments) to their names when they came up with the technically advanced HP 200A resistance capacity audio oscillator. The HP 200A was an instrument used to test sound equipment, and The Walt Disney Company snagged them both a patent as well as a contract. The studio's ensuing order for eight HP 200As, and their part in the development of its groundbreaking film *Fantasia*, started the Hewlett-Packard Company on a regular path of innovative electronics excellence.

Right from the beginning, though, Hewlett and Packard also recognized the importance of their relationship with employees. They focused their creative energies there as well. The two built facilities with an open floor plan—including executive offices without doors—and established an official "Open Door Policy" to help establish mutual trust at all levels. They additionally implemented their now-famous "Management by Walking Around" philosophy to actively engage supervisors and workers in even more deliberate and meaningful ways.

During the 1950s, significant breakthroughs continued on both the product and personnel fronts. Successful releases, such as the HP 524A high-speed frequency counter, a device used by radio stations to comply with certain federal regulations, rolled out of their increasingly busy plant. Profits were reinvested in new research and development, freeing the partners from venture capitalists and resultant debt. The practice also allowed them to acquire a plotter company that would eventually form the basis for their printer business. And it gave them the footing to go public.

At the same time, HP's progressive philosophies helped it attract top young scientists and engineers. In 1957, the company formalized its unique objectives and management style in "The HP Way." The following year, it split into separate divisions with individual profit-and-loss accountability, and moved them out of headquarters in Palo Alto. Each became a self-sustaining unit responsible for developing, manufacturing, and marketing its own products—and would be awarded future R&D funding in direct proportion to performance. In 1959, HP took these ideas global and opened a manufacturing facility in Germany and a European headquarters in Switzerland. It also made stock-option plans a part of its employee benefits package, and became the first company to institute a cash profit-sharing program.

The 1960s was a decade of flex time and calculators. The former first appeared in HP's German plant in 1967, and time clocks completely disappeared throughout the company within a half-dozen years. The latter hit the market in 1968 in the form of the HP 9100, proudly proclaimed by the company to this day as the world's first programmable scientific desktop calculator. (Four years later, HP would introduce its first handheld version, the HP 35. Slide rules suddenly became superfluous, and the technology revolution went portable.)

The company also entered the world of business computing in 1972 with the HP 3000 minicomputer. By this time, it had 16,000 employees and sales of more than $365 million. Only top college graduates were recruited for the expanding workforce. They were retained by the challenging professional atmosphere, and the progressive people programs that now included a strict promote-from-within policy and an unofficial ban on layoffs.

Desktop mainframe computers were unveiled with the now-familiar Hewlett-Packard logo in the early 1980s, and the company entered the printing business in 1984. Its reasonably priced inkjet and laser printers took the market by storm and quickly became ubiquitous. Concurrently, the company formed four "sector" organizations to manage its proliferating groups while establishing the first high-tech joint venture in China. When it celebrated its 50th anniversary in 1989, the garage where Hewlett and Packard developed that first audio oscillator was designated a California State Historical Landmark.

By the mid-1990s, HP's diversified units had introduced breakthrough products—ranging from a palm-sized PC weighing 11 ounces to a device that processed ultrasound waves for noninvasive real-time cardiac analysis. It teamed up with Intel to develop a common 64-bit microprocessor architecture and moved vigorously into the growing home-office market. It also formalized policies on telecommuting which encouraged employees to work at home or remote offices around the globe. Half of all sales were now coming from outside the United States—10 percent of the world's high-tech retail space featured its products. And by the end of the decade, the original garage startup had grown into a major multinational with 104 divisions, 19,000 products, and more than $47 billion in sales.

Yet growth, which once regularly hit 20 percent a year, was virtually nonexistent. HP stock was flagging, despite a bull market that had been particularly kind to tech companies. No new business lines were emerging, but strong competitors certainly were. And the Internet appeared an afterthought while key executives routinely fielded offers from outside. In response, the company long known for its unorthodox ways responded with some very radical changes.

The transformation actually began under former CEO Lew Platt, who took the helm as HP's fourth leader in 1992. Platt, considered a capable manager but not an innovator, realized things needed to change and began the corporate makeover just a few years later. Much like IBM, he decided to reinvent HP as an Internet solutions company providing hardware, software, and support for corporate customers. He also decided that the company's decentralized nature was stifling its attempts to move on "Internet time," and he realigned it into two cohesive operations: Agilent Technologies, a new $8 billion company selling test-and-measurement equipment and medical electronics, and a $40 billion company selling computers, printers, software and services that bore the long-standing Hewlett-Packard name. Platt further announced that he would be stepping down early at the end of 1999, and that the new HP would be led by a new CEO.

Carly Fiorina, who managed the original branding campaign that helped Lucent gain respect in the industry and get noticed by Wall Street, was one of 100 candidates for the slot. When chosen after an array of tests (which reportedly included a three-hour interview and a 900-question psychological survey), Fiorina immediately leapt into the fray with her characteristic high-energy zeal. Within days, she was meeting with supporters as well as detractors inside the company and out. She quickly tallied $1 billion in savings by consolidating diverse operations, and considered layoffs that observers estimated could ultimately pare the payroll by 25 percent. She reoriented the company's disparate advertising and marketing approaches, lent her own voice to commercials in a radical departure from HP's long-time publicity shy ways, altered product designs, and announced entirely new lines, such as digital cameras, a printer that allows bookstores to rapidly produce entire books on demand, and software that provides intriguing possibilities of electronic commerce. She also dropped the venerable "Hewlett-Packard" logo off many of them in favor of a more trendy "HP."

For a company so immersed in tradition that it keeps official corporate artifacts tended by a full-time archivist, this whirlwind of activity—all accomplished or announced within months of Fiorina's hiring—was quite jarring, to say the least. But it's nothing less than the promise voiced in one of her first national TV spots: "The original startup will act like one again. Watch."

23

Standard Oil Company

Fact File:

✓ Founders: John D. Rockefeller, Samuel Andrews, and Henry M. Flagler
✓ Distinction: World's largest oil refiner before dismantling by Supreme Court.
✓ Primary products: Kerosene, fuel, lubricant, other petroleum by-products.
✓ Founder and president: John D. Rockefeller.
✓ Founding location: Cleveland, Ohio.
✓ Market balue before dissolution: $100 million.
✓ Major competitors: None.
✓ Years in Existence: 1870-1911.

Whenever anyone mentions the Standard Oil Company, two things immediately spring to mind: Rockefeller and monopoly. The linkage is unavoidable, for nobody but John D. Rockefeller could have built this oil refining goliath—and nothing but a charge of monopoly could have torn it down. Further, the three are forever intertwined because all reached their zenith in an era when the industrial revolution was transforming American business into the global force it remains to this day.

Rockefeller didn't run this gargantuan enterprise on his own, of course. Even a titan of his stature required an extraordinary management team to handle the so-called "octopus" of the refinery industry, which at its peak controlled almost all U.S. oil production, processing, marketing and transportation. But it was J.D., as he was known, who put it all together and ran it. Until, that is, he and his company ran afoul of the federal anti-trust laws that eventually shut them down.

But Rockefeller was more than one of the most astute businessmen of his time. Rockefeller's estate was worth about $1 billion when he died at age 97—a sum that would be 10 times that today. A lifelong philanthropist, he gave away money even when he barely had any. He donated $20,000 to help build Cleveland's Euclid Avenue Baptist Church the year Standard Oil was born. Over the next seven decades he also financed the Rockefeller Foundation and Rockefeller Institute for Medical Research, among other charities, while funding the University of Chicago and presenting countless additional gifts to many more colleges and churches. During the course of his life, in fact, he gave away an estimated $500 million in philanthropic gifts. Yet these days he is primarily remembered by many, and none too fondly at that, for the infamous oil refinery from which he made his fortune.

From most accounts of his remarkable life, however, it is apparent that this contradiction never bothered him much.

John Davison Rockefeller was born on a farm in upstate New York in 1839. One of four children, he was raised by a very religious mother while his father was busy swindling locals with financial con games and phony medical cures. When J.D. was 10, his father was accused of raping a household worker and the family fled. Eventually, they wound up in Cleveland. Not long after, the elder Rockefeller ran off to South Dakota on his own.

J.D. landed his first job in 1855, working as an assistant bookkeeper for the Hewitt & Tuttle commodities house. He earned $3.50 a week and donated regularly to his church. Nonetheless, he managed to save $800 in just three years. With that and a small borrowed stake, he and a British immigrant named Maurice B. Clark opened a commodities business of their own. The firm, which dealt in hay, grain, meats, and other goods, prospered.

Rockefeller was only 19, but he was restless to expand. Oil was then a booming industry, and had been since a successful well was sunk in Pennsylvania's Allegheny mountains about 10 years earlier. Clark had a friend in the business, and in 1863 he came to the pair seeking funds. Rockefeller invested $4,000 and took his first step into the field that was to make him rich.

The exploration and drilling for petroleum always has been an up-and-down business. It certainly was no different in those days, when a barrel fetched anywhere from 10 cents to $20. By the time Rockefeller entered the fray, the price was fluctuating around $5. But that wasn't what really interested him. Rockefeller was savvy enough to recognize that when drillers did make a successful strike, they needed refiners to produce and market the resulting by-products. He also realized that there was much more money to be made on this end. So, with Clark and a new partner named Samuel Andrews, he formed a small Ohio refinery in 1863 and dubbed it Excelsior Oil Works.

With growth on its mind, the new company began buying other existing refineries. It quickly picked up 50 in Cleveland, and another 80 in Pittsburgh. Sensing that profits would be even greater if they controlled all aspects of their operation, the partners also started purchasing warehouses, timber stands (to make their own barrels), and even fleets of ships (to transport the products they produced). In 1865 Rockefeller bought out Clark's interests and two years later brought in local businessman Henry Flagler, who had money and the inside track in an emerging transport mode—railroads—that would prove even more important to their industry than ships. They renamed the company Rockefeller, Andrews & Flagler. It evolved into Standard Oil within three years, and soon could legitimately claim to be the largest operation of its kind in the world.

Standard initially had competition both domestically and overseas. The Nobel Brothers of Sweden and Britain's Shell Transport & Trading, for example, were a large reason why America had captured just over half of all global production by the late 1880s. But Standard continually hired the top chemists, marketing specialists, attorneys, and other professionals. It also, according to most accounts, closed secret deals with companies it needed and strong-armed those it did not. Standard Oil rapidly grew in size as well as profitability. Eventually, it was the exclusive supplier of petroleum products to some 37,000 communities.

🌍🌍🌍

The late 19th century was a period of astounding change in American business. Cities sprang up almost overnight and railroads tied them together. Manufacturing became the dominant force in the U.S. economy, and a handful of individuals— Andrew Carnegie, Cornelius Vanderbilt, J.P. Morgan, and Rockefeller, among them— controlled the most powerful companies leading the way. These men were resourceful and imaginative, and sometimes not opposed to pulling any strings necessary to stay atop their respective fields. Because most states at the time prohibited local companies from holding shares in others headquartered outside their borders, Rockefeller devised a way around the applicable laws in order to expand. In 1882, he formed the Standard Oil Trust to combine Standard with affiliated companies in other locations. Utilizing a maze of obscure legal devices that made the structure difficult to decipher, it brought some 40 corporations under his authority and continued to exercise ironclad control in its industry.

Charges of illegal rebates, coercive tactics, and predatory pricing continued to mount. In 1892 the Ohio Supreme Court stepped into the fray and ordered the trust dissolved. Undaunted, Rockefeller continued operating from his New York headquarters. In 1899, when states began relaxing their incorporation statutes, he reorganized as the Standard Oil of New Jersey holding company and transferred all assets to this new entity.

Rockefeller's actions did not go unnoticed by other industrialists. Some forged similar trusts in the cotton, whiskey, sugar, and tobacco industries. Others consummated megamergers that created corporate giants such as General Electric, AT&T,

and U.S. Steel. These vast concentrations of wealth and power increasingly struck observers (and would-be competitors) as unfair, if not downright criminal. Journalists began taking notice and one—Ida M. Tarbell—put Standard under the microscope in a 19-part expose that appeared in a *McClure's* magazine beginning in 1902. In issue after issue, Tarbell hammered at Rockefeller's claims that his corporation did nothing untoward. Rather, she wrote, Standard Oil's rise to prominence was "accomplished by fraud, deceit, special privilege, gross illegality, bribery, coercion, corruption, intimidation, espionage, or outright terror."

The series made Tarbell a celebrity, with President Theodore Roosevelt among her many fans. (Rockefeller offered no comment, but reportedly savaged the writer in private conversations.) The series also initiated a federal investigation, and in 1906 the government filed suit under its 16-year-old Sherman Anti-Trust Act. This officially alleged what long had been whispered: that Standard Oil monopolized the oil industry, and thereby restricted free trade.

In 1907, the company was found in violation of antitrust laws and fined about one-third of its $100 million market value. That penalty was thrown out, but a little more than four years later—on May 15, 1911—the U.S. Supreme Court ruled that Standard's structure was indeed "a monopoly in restraint of trade" and ordered it split into some three dozen separate companies. Rockefeller was out on the golf course when he heard the news, and reportedly advised his playing partners to "buy Standard Oil." It proved a wise tip, as the pieces of his empire soon were worth far more than the single entity ever had been. Rockefeller's own considerable fortune soared to even greater heights, and later that year he retired.

The breakup created many names that to this day are well-known in the oil business, including Exxon, Amoco, Mobil, and Chevron. It long remained controversial, though, as many suspected that Standard might have escaped its fate had Rockefeller been more politically astute—or more willing to kowtow to regulators and officials. (Although it was equally in control of its own industry, for example, the contemporary U.S. Steel did not similarly fall victim to antitrust regulations.) But Rockefeller was never one to genuflect to secular powers, or shrink from the doctrine under which he lived his life. "I believe it is a religious duty to get all the money you can, fairly and honestly; to keep all you can, and to give away all you can," he once said. When he died in 1937, no one could dispute that he ever doubted what he was doing. Or that he hadn't followed those beliefs unerringly to the end.

32

Procter & Gamble Co.

Fact File:

✓ Founders: William Procter and James Gamble.
✓ Distinction: Made its name in soaps; invented soap operas to promote them.
✓ Primary products: Cleaning, paper, beauty, food, health-care items.
✓ Annual sales: $38.125 billion.
✓ Number of employees: 110,000.
✓ Major competitors: Johnson & Johnson, Kimberly-Clark, Unilever.
✓ Chairman: John E. Pepper; President and CEO: Alan G. Lafley.
✓ Headquarters: Cincinnati, Ohio.
✓ Year founded: 1837.
✓ Web site: www.pg.com.

Since Andrew Jackson was president, Procter & Gamble has been ubiquitous. Today, the world's dominant consumer-products company peddles a dizzying array of household goods under 300 brand names in 140 countries—and an astounding number are truly household names: Tide, Camay, Crest, Scope, Secret, Clearasil, Folgers, Crisco, Pringles, Pepto-Bismol, Vicks VapoRub, Old Spice, Oil of Olay, Head & Shoulders, Spic and Span, Pampers, Tampax, Charmin....The list goes on. And on.

Founded on the production of soap and candles by two immigrants from the British Isles who landed in Cincinnati, P&G long ago abandoned the latter in favor of paper, beauty, healthcare, food and beverage products. It continues focusing, though, on the laundry and cleaning items that evolved from its first widespread success: Ivory soap. And always the innovator—the company was first to offer synthetic detergent, fluoride toothpaste, and disposable diapers—it forged into the

21st century with an abundance of new-and-improved variations on its now familiar themes. Products such as an at-home dry cleaning kit, low-fat snack foods, and a cleanser for fruits and vegetables regularly spring from its laboratories.

P&G became number-one in such items in the United States, and expanded globally so that half of all sales are now derived abroad. They prevail by designing products (and a corporation itself) that are distinctive. Nearly as important, it utilized omnipresent and often original marketing programs to consistently spread their word. P&G, after all, has spent lavishly on print ads for more than a century, and it began airing television commercials only five months after that medium's debut. It also used radio to push products as early as 1923. And 10 years later produced the first "soap opera" to exclusively hawk Oxydol—creating a programming staple it later transferred successfully to TV, where its *Guiding Light* and *As the World Turns* serials remain popular.

But the company has not initially found its third century as inviting as its first two. Like many other Old Economy pioneers, it has been slow to embrace the Internet. And when revenues were not as strong as expected, its market value plummeted $36 billion in one horrendous day. Rightly or wrongly, observers feared that P&G's streak of innovation and growth may finally have hit a wall.

Much like a surprising number of their contemporaries, candlemaker William Procter and soapmaker James Gamble came to create a lasting business by serendipitous accident. Procter, from England, and Gamble, from Ireland, were each on their way out West when they stopped in the busy commercial and industrial center of Cincinnati to tend to personal matters. The two eventually married sisters, and their mutual father-in-law suggested that the young men start a business. In 1937, they signed a formal partnership agreement, kicked in $3,596.47 apiece, and opened the Procter & Gamble soap and candle company.

Despite shaky economic times and more than a dozen competitors in Cincinnati alone, the business boomed. By 1859 it employed 80 and recorded its first million in sales. To meet demand it built a new plant even as the Civil War approached, which paid off handsomely when it helped fulfill a contract to supply Union armies with its two main products. It paid off yet again when soldiers took positive memories of P&G home with with them after the war.

James Norris Gamble, a trained chemist and the son of one founder, developed an inexpensive white soap that eventually would become the company's signature product and first big hit. Harley Procter, the other founder's son, dubbed it "Ivory" when a Biblical passage he came across seemed to sum up its qualities. He then convinced the partners to shell out $11,000—a preposterous sum at the time—to advertise its purity and buoyant properties across the country. P&G's business again skyrocketed, and additional facilities were again needed.

Unlike all but a few businesses of the day, this company additionally recognized that its welfare was directly linked to that of its workforce. Accordingly, in 1885 it began giving employees Saturday afternoons off—with pay. In 1886, it opened its new Ivorydale factory with the latest technological advances designed to improve the working environment. In 1887 it instituted a profit-sharing plan. Ultimately, it also became one of the first firms to provide its personnel with comprehensive insurance programs.

By the end of the 19th century, P&G was selling 30 varieties of soap. The partners incorporated to finance even more expansion. Although the imminent arrival of the light bulb would soon spell doom for the candle trade, additional manufacturing facilities were constructed in Kansas City and Ontario, Canada. A newly opened research lab developed items such as Dreft, the first synthetic detergent, and Crisco, the first all-vegetable shortening. Color print ads were used to market the soaps, and a nationwide cooking show on radio was used to market the shortening. To maintain momentum, P&G formed one of the business world's first market-research departments.

Between the two World Wars, Procter & Gamble prospered as much as any American firm. It regularly unveiled new products that constantly struck a chord with the buying public, established an overseas subsidiary in England, and expanded into Asia. It sponsored its first radio serial (*Ma Perkins*), entered the hair-care business with its first shampoo, and aired a TV commercial during the very first televised major league baseball game. Around the time of its 100th anniversary, it also reached $230 million in annual sales.

The following period was marked by even more impressive growth. Much of it was funded by the success of Tide laundry detergent, which was introduced in 1946. Within four years, it became the runaway best-seller in its burgeoning category. Prell shampoo, Crest toothpaste, Duncan Hines cake mixes, and Charmin toilet tissue, towels, and napkins were also added to the corporate roster around that time. In 1961, P&G really shook up the consumer world with Pampers, the first-ever disposable diaper. During the next few years existing categories were strengthened with the acquisition of Folgers coffee, the invention of Bounce fabric-softening sheets, and the development of successful pharmaceutical products. P&G also began building new manufacturing facilities in Mexico, Europe, and Japan.

By 1980, as it approached its 150th anniversary, the company was doing business in 23 countries and recording nearly $11 billion in annual sales. Cosmetics and fragrances entered the picture in a big way through the acquisitions of Max Factor and Noxell's Cover Girl, Noxzema, and Clarion lines. The healthcare division expanded with the purchase of Norwich Eaton Pharmaceuticals and Richardson-Vicks. Overseas business was bolstered in Eastern Europe and China. By the time sales hit $30 billion in 1993, more than 50 percent of sales were generated outside the United States.

Procter & Gamble also continued its long-time people- and community-friendly ways, regularly racking up awards for its socially conscious behavior even as it grew to its huge multinational status. Its many accolades include a Johns Hopkins-School of Public Health acknowledgment for using alternatives to animal research; recognition by various specialized magazines as a top employment environment for Hispanics, executive women, and working mothers; a World Environment Center Gold Medal for international corporate environmental achievement; and the U.S. Labor Department's Opportunity 2000 Award for its commitment to equal employment and a diverse workforce.

But despite even more strategic acquisitions (such as Tambrands and its category-leading Tampax tampon) and innovative introductions (such as salty snacks fried in fat-free, calorie-free Olean cooking oil), nearly 17 decades of consistent success came to a crashing halt on March 7, 2000, when P&G stock dropped 31 percent in a single day.

The news stunned Wall Street: within minutes of the New York Stock Exchange opening bell, Procter & Gamble fell $27.0625 to $60.375—and that came on top of its ongoing collapse from a high of $117 just six months earlier. The bluest of blue chips, the oldest of the biggest in the *Fortune* 500, P&G had announced a 10-percent drop in profits after earnings forecasters predicted a 7- to 9-percent increase. Management blamed rising prices for raw materials, such as petroleum and wood pulp, belated results from a reorganization the year before, and higher costs related to federal approvals in its pharmaceuticals division. Wondering why none of this was anticipated earlier, investors worried that another shoe could yet drop.

Not since Phillip Morris' stock slid 23 percent in 1993 had a major company collapsed so dramatically and so decisively. Many blamed P&G's newly appointed top executive, Durk Jager, who had perhaps bitten off more than he could chew by trying simultaneously to change the company's notoriously insular culture, introduce a slew of new products, and initiate even more acquisitions.

P&G was also scored for moving slow to the Internet, and for its tardiness in hooking up with major retailers to develop popular private-label brands of detergent and other products. Some analysts and investors expressed continuing fears about the company's future, and when weak earnings were again projected for the fourth quarter of 2000, Jager suddenly and unexpectedly announced his retirement effective July 1. He was replaced as president and chief executive by Alan Lafley, president of P&Gs divisions for global beauty care in North America. John Pepper, who ran the company before Jager, was named chairman.

Citing P&G's considerable strengths—the fact that it virtually invented the now-hot concepts of branding and brand marketing, for instance, and its unparalleled stable of worldwide household names—many observers say it's far too early to count this bellwether corporation out of the game. Recovery will take work, they note, but nearly 180 years of experience should count for something.

soft AT&T Ford Apple McDonald's America Online FedEx CBS Philip Morris Wal-Mart Ger
ric IBM Sears Roebuck Motors J.P. Morgan & Co. Union Pacific RCA Nike Intel CNN Boeing Hew
ard Standard Oil Sony USX-U.S. Steel Group Agence France-Presse Levitt & Sons Walt Dis
ape Coca-Co Thyssen Krupp Proctor & Gamble Yahoo! Toyota People Express Manpower Toys
National Footb ague Kell Johnson Publishing Firestone Tire & Rubber Avon Products H
s Ben omem AX Singer Sewing Shorebank Corp. Metro-Goldwyn-Mayer L.L. E
Heinz Microsoft AT&T Ford Apple McDonald's America Online FedEx CBS Philip Morris Wal-M
ral Electric IBM Sears Roebuck Motors J.P. Morgan & Co. Union Pacific RCA Nike Intel CNN Bo
tt-Packard Standard Oil Sony USX-U.S. Steel Group France-Presse Sons Walt Dis
ape Coca-Cola Thyssen Krupp Proctor & Gamble Toyc
National Football League Kellogg Johnson Publishing Firestone Tire & Rubber Avon Products H
s Ben & Jerry's Homemade

Number

33

Yahoo! Inc.

Fact File:

✓ Founders: David Filo and Jerry Yang.
✓ Distinction: The original online search engine;
  now profitable Internet portal.
✓ Primary Products: Web directory, chat, shopping, community functions.
✓ Annual Sales: $588.6 million.
✓ Number of Employees: 2,711.
✓ Major Competitors: America Online, Lycos, Microsoft.
✓ Chairman and CEO: Timothy Koogle;
  Chief Yahoos!: Jerry Yang, David Filo.
✓ Headquarters: Santa Clara, Calif.
✓ Year Founded: 1994.
✓ Web site: www.yahoo.com.

W hen the Web was still a primitive but tantalizing novelty for the few nerds and hackers clever enough to finagle early access, there was just one way to navigate its already vast and mysterious terrain: Yahoo! The wonderfully odd (yet strangely appropriate) exclamatory moniker quickly came to define the Web's first "search engine." It was a straightforward but artfully compiled online directory that attracted experienced as well as novice visitors. They could easily locate any type of site—or any specific one—and travel there instantly by means of a single mouse click. This may sound like standard fare today, but back in the mid-1990s, it was downright amazing.

Meeting a booming demand as it did, Yahoo! grew fast. The company went from a dorm room in 1994, to incorporation in 1995, to initial public offering in

1996. Regional and other highly focused offshoots, such as a kid's guide, were added regularly. Customer conveniences, including news, sports and business headlines, e-mail and assorted online services, chat rooms and message boards, electronic shopping and auctions, soon followed. Advertisers were signed to pay for it all, while the continually escalating traffic rapidly made it profitable—and even more of a standout in its field.

Today, the Yahoo! brand is one of the most established in cyberspace. Founders Jerry Yang and David Filo have each realized about $7.5 billion from the venture. Their firm, in which they retain active roles, now calls itself "a global Internet communications, commerce, and media corporation." From headquarters in California and offices in Europe, the Asian Pacific basin, Latin America, and Canada, it serves nearly 50 million Web travelers each month and contracts with about 5,200 advertisers and partners who foot the bills...and then some.

And yet, as Yahoo! and the Internet both prepare for the new century, it is still running hard to maintain its place among powerful competitors, such as AOL and Microsoft. However, that incredibly extensive, and remarkably effective, Web directory still assembled primarily by human editors who apply a logic and execution all their own evolves as mighty new technologies impact its core.

Jerry Yang, born in Taiwan in 1968, moved to the United States 10 years later as part of the first group of immigrants permitted into the country after diplomatic relations were reestablished with China. He, his university professor mother, and younger brother wound up in San Jose. Although the kids were initially at a distinct disadvantage when it came to the language, they excelled at math from their arrival. In short order they also conquered English. By the time Yang graduated from high school he was class valedictorian (as well as student body president). He accepted a scholarship to Stanford, and in four years earned both a bachelor's and master's degree in engineering.

David Filo, two years older than Yang, was raised in Louisiana before earning his bachelor's degree from Tulane. The two met in 1989 when Filo moved to Palo Alto to attend Stanford's graduate school. Much like Yang, he pursued a Ph.D. in electrical engineering. Learning they shared a passion for sports, in addition to a few more technical pursuits, the pair became more friendly three years later while on a six-month academic exchange program in Japan. Upon their return, the campus was abuzz over the newly available World Wide Web and a software application called Mosaic that offered rudimentary access to a seemingly endless sea of computer files. Captivated, Yang and Filo decided to do some work in the new medium.

Their first effort combined Mosaic and a software program they concocted to amass and sort statistical data on players in the National Basketball Association. Yang also designed some early Web sites, including one dedicated to sumo wrestling. After about a year, the two were among those noticing how difficult it had become to negotiate the ever-growing online world. So, starting with a purely academic goal—locating research papers at universities around the globe—they built a program to organize Web sites into appropriate categories. The site they developed to showcase them, originally called Jerry's Guide to the World Wide Web, went online in April 1994. It was soon renamed Yahoo!, which, according to corporate lore, stands for "Yet Another Hierarchical Officious Oracle." Just as likely, though, the name was picked because it sounded goofy and had plenty of anti-establishment connotations.

As usage increased, Yang and Filo worked day and night to convert their system into a customized database that could be accessed by even more people. It originally resided on their own workstations—Yang's "akebono" and Filo's "konishiki," (both named after sumo wrestlers). Before long their traffic was straining Stanford's electronic infrastructure. The two began looking for someplace to relocate, and in early 1995 accepted an offer from Netscape Communications co-founder Marc Andreessen to move their files to larger computers housed at his company's nearby Mountain View headquarters. To further emphasize that Yahoo! was now a serious business, the company incorporated on March 5 of that year. Along with employee number three, another student named Tim Brady, the founders also put together a business plan and began to seek funding.

One key to Yahoo!'s success, then as now, has been its incorporation of a human touch into the otherwise mechanical process of selecting and categorizing site listings. Another has been its long-standing decision to skip complicated (and computer-crashing) graphics in favor of simple (and quick loading) basic text interrupted only by the banner ads that pay the bills. Yang and Filo also suspected from the start that Yahoo! could become much more than a directory or "search engine." It could, they believed, become a major entry point for all Web visitors. Venture capitalists agreed, and Yahoo! picked up $1 million to put its plan in motion. Tim Koogle, who graduated from Stanford about 15 years before Yang and Filo and then ran a $400 million company called Intermec, met with the pair for a Sunday night interview at a brewpub in Mountain View. He accepted their offer on the spot to become Yahoo!'s CEO.

The team, which remains intact to this day, immediately set about making their company profitable. Nobody knew then whether an advertising-based business was even feasible on the Net, but they tried it for a quarter and it worked. In response, they decided to go public and prove that what they were doing could be very profitable indeed. On April 11, 1996, the company completed its initial public offering and raised an astounding $35.043 million.

Now it was time to see what Yahoo! really could do. Working with a disproportionately small staff—much like most Internet companies—they created features that drove more and more visitors to the site. They added regional and specialized guides, stock quotes and sports scores, recipes, and shopping. They acquired GeoCities, a company that lets individuals create personalized Web sites; *Broadcast.com*, a broadband technology that allows Yahoo! to transmit original shows such as *FinanceVision* (a live business program that delivers market news throughout the day); and Online

Anywhere, which enables cell phones, Palm Pilots, and other electronic gadgets to access the Web.

As the founders predicted, Yahoo! has indeed become a top Internet portal. Every month, two-thirds of all online visitors click over to the site. Yahoo! has astutely leveraged these visitors by matching the banner ads they see with their personal interests and general demographics. Through such tactics, it has remained profitable since the fourth quarter of 1996. But even as investors clamor for a piece of the action, and its market capitalization tops $90 billion—higher than that of Ford or General Motors—Chief Yahoos! Yang and Filo, and CEO Koogle, must constantly seek new ways to keep it atop the cyber-heap.

The new millenium brought new challenges to Yahoo!, not the least of which accompanied long-time archrival America Online's blockbuster announcement that it was acquiring Time Warner Inc. and thus creating the world's largest entertainment and communications conglomerate. But even as other online competitors like Infoseek also teamed up with other traditional media companies such as The Walt Disney Company—providing access to deep economic and content resources, as well as a huge customer base—Yahoo! continued its strategy of partnering with many companies instead of buying a big one. In 1999, for example, it enhanced its e-tailing capabilities by teaming with Kmart to create *BlueLight.com* and offer online shopping and free Internet access to the brick-and-mortar chain's millions of shoppers.

Having come somewhat late to online shopping, Yahoo! now pursues it aggressively. Rather than selling merchandise directly, however, it teams up with others (such as Kmart) and charges a fee for all transactions originating from its site. It has also hooked up with Ford to provide online services for the automaker's future models, and with four specialized firms to tackle the potentially huge arena of business-to-business sales.

The tactics seem to be working, as earnings continue beating analysts' expectations and share prices remain healthy. The company reported a record 680 million page views per day on average during June 2000, while the number of registered users worldwide passed 156 million. It has moved into new headquarters in Santa Clara, Calif., where the cubicles are splashed with purple and yellow. A classic Ford Fairlane in the same colors sits parked out front, and the conference rooms are all named for flavors of Ben & Jerry's ice cream.

Like it has throughout its brief but influential history, Yahoo! continues reaching boldly for the future while keeping one foot planted firmly in its goofy, antiestablishment past.

34

Toyota Motor Company

Fact File:

✓ Founder: Sakichi Toyoda.
✓ Distinction: Revolutionized automobile production for the global age.
✓ Primary products: Cars, pickups, minivans and SUVs.
✓ Annual sales: $105.832 billion.
✓ Number of employees: 183,879.
✓ Major competitors: DaimlerChrysler, Ford, General Motors.
✓ Honorary chairman: Shoichiro Toyoda; Chairman: Hiroshi Okuda; President: Fujio Cho.
✓ Headquarters: Toyota City, Japan.
✓ Year founded: 1937.
✓ Web site: www.toyota.com.

W hen Eiji Toyoda first came to Detroit as a brash young engineer in 1950, Ford was producing 8,000 vehicles a day and his own family-run auto business in Japan was turning out just 40. A half century later, his business—which actually started as a textile mill—has grown into an international conglomerate that manufactures cars in 24 countries and markets them in 160. Like others in its home nation, however, the company has experienced significant setbacks of late. But much as Eiji Toyoda saw only opportunities when he examined the competition during that first trip to the United States, his predecessors see innumerable opportunities remaining today.

Toyota Motors, as the company was subtly renamed just before that Motown visit, is now Japan's biggest carmaker and the fourth largest in the world. A multi-dimensional behemoth, it sells more than $100 billion worth of automobiles, automotive parts, industrial equipment and prefabricated housing every year. Its gas-powered cars, pickups, minivans and SUVs carry some of the top nameplates in the industry, such as Camry, Land Cruiser, and various ritzy monikers in the upscale Lexus line. It is now also producing the closely watched Prius, a five-seater sedan powered by a much heralded new hybrid gas-and-electric engine.

Yet times are tougher at Toyota than they have been in decades. Eiji Toyoda saw what large-scale production could accomplish when he stepped into that Ford plant some 50 years ago. In partnership with his cousin Kiichiro (and Kiichiro's son, Shoichiro, currently the company's honorary chairman), he helped adapt it for a new era. The moves identified Toyota as one of the most innovative companies in the world, and helped make it one of the most successful. But in recent years it has been losing market share. Capital is drying up. Younger buyers find its offerings old-fashioned. And the company that wrote the book on auto manufacturing in the global era may be in danger of suffering the same fate as other once-pioneering operations. Insiders can be excused if they aren't unduly worried, however; they've seen similar negatives turn positive before.

Cousins Eiji and Kiichiro Toyoda spent much of their youth in the family's textile mill in western Japan. Established as the Toyoda Spinning & Weaving Company in 1918, its fate relied largely on the ingenuity of Sakichi Toyoda—Kiichiro's father and Eiji's uncle—who for decades had been tinkering with looms to improve their efficiency. When a British textile concern offered an impressive sum in 1929 for the rights to his latest, the Toyoda family saw an opportunity to shift gears entirely and convert to automobile production.

Ford and General Motors were already assembling some vehicles in Japan, but Sakichi Toyoda had visions of a true Japanese car. Kiichiro helped set up the family's new manufacturing operation, while Eiji was sent off to Tokyo Imperial University to study mechanical engineering. In 1934, the Toyodas produced an engine so identical to a Chevrolet model it accepted Chevrolet parts. Under Kiichiro's leadership it also found revolutionary ways to boost efficiency. Improved factory design was one. A new system of material supply—in which parts were delivered to the assembly line only as they were needed, or "just in time" as the widely copied practice is called today—was another.

After receiving his degree in 1936, Eiji returned to the business. The family's first passenger car, the Model AA, was to go into production that same year. But the Japanese government needed trucks for its nascent war effort, so the Toyodas switched modes again and were soon producing 1,000 a month. Supplies dwindled as the military campaign faltered, however, and truck production dwindled as well. Then, on the day immediately before the War ended, a bomb destroyed a large portion of the family plant in what is now Toyota City.

As the Toyodas were wondering what business ideas they should next pursue (fish paste and chinaware were among those considered) U.S. occupational forces asked them to manufacture buses and trucks to aid the post-war recovery. Kiichiro, Eiji, and Shoichiro rebuilt their plant and resumed production, but promised payments failed to materialize. To win support from nervous creditors, Eiji created a separate company to coordinate orders, deliveries, and payments. He visited Detroit to study the competition, and came away with inspiration and ideas. He also developed his first yearning for international expansion, which led to exports to a half-dozen countries including the United States by the end of the decade.

Innovations up and down the line—usually aiming for efficiencies similar to those achieved by Sakichi Toyoda's original looms—culminated on New Year's Day 1955 when Toyota's first passenger auto, the Crown, was driven from the plant by a tuxedo-clad Eiji Toyoda. It quickly proved popular in Japan, but not in America where it was introduced two years later. The Toyodas once again retooled, though, and came back in 1960 with the Corona. This model became a huge seller in the United States, and put Toyota on the automaking map.

By deploying assorted labor-conserving strategies, the company smoothly increased production to meet demand. By implementing various unconventional management practices—such as encouraging assembly line personnel to catch and correct all defects on the spot—it continually improved its reputation along with its operation. For these and other forward-thinking practices, Toyota was awarded the prestigious Deming Prize in 1965. It was rewarded in a more tangible way in 1966 when its second mass-produced model, the Corolla, became an instant hit upon release in the United States. The following year, Eiji Toyoda was named to head the company.

Toyota now had solid products to go with experienced leadership and trailblazing ideas. And in the 1970s it got something new: Huge gasoline price hikes. This suddenly made its tradition-laden Detroit competition look a lot less attractive. Americans turned in droves to the smaller fuel-efficient cars offered by Toyota and a smattering of others such as Datsun (later renamed Nissan) and Honda. Car buyers in Japan also were increasingly choosing Toyota, which remained under the day-to-day leadership of Eiji Toyoda until 1982. (By tradition he then moved over to the company's Board of Directors, where he sat until 1994. That year, at age 81, he was enshrined in the U.S. Automotive Hall of Fame near his long-time idol Henry Ford.)

U.S. automakers, stung by the insurgents, hit back with a page or two from Toyoda's own book. They introduced Japanese-style inventory control, for example, and started programs to increase worker-management unity. And then the giant, General Motors, stepped completely out of the box by building a subcompact in cooperation with Toyota. It was modeled on the Corolla, and assembled at a shuttered GM plant in California with half of all parts—including the engine and drive train—made by Toyota in Japan. Many observers initially doubted the partnership would work, and newspaper accounts called it "improbable." Nonetheless, when the resultant $7,195 Chevrolet Nova debuted in 1985, it found instant support among both value-conscious "buy American" consumers and those who by now staunchly preferred imports.

Toyota's remarkable ascendance continued throughout the decade. GM—which once dismissed it, along with fellow Japanese automakers, as merely a purveyor of flimsy little cars who got lucky during the oil crisis—saw its U.S. market share drop from nearly one-half to one-third despite repeated remedial efforts. Toyota, on the other hand, boosted its slice of the pie considerably by introducing the pricey Lexus line in 1989. It also kept turning out appealing new models and smart updates for its long-time audience. The combination helped it sell more than 1 million vehicles in the United States, and capture 43 percent of all car sales in Japan. In 1990, *Fortune* magazine acknowledged that Toyota was "the best carmaker in the world."

It couldn't last, of course. By the mid-1990s car buyers in Japan were increasingly turning to imports, just as those in America had done two decades earlier. In the United States, Toyota was caught unprepared as consumer tastes shifted toward minivans and sport utility vehicles. In Europe and China, it still lagged badly behind other manufacturers. And the Asian economy itself was about to tank, sending sales of everything—especially cars—into a tailspin.

With that backdrop, Hiroshi Okuda was named president in 1995. The 63-year-old Okuda, who had been with Toyota for 41 years, felt substantial changes were immediately needed. He launched a major advertising campaign at home, vigorously attacked the company's onerous cost structure, and got even busier updating and redesigning. Okuda, considered a "new generation" business leader in Japan, also speculated that the telecommunications or housing industries would one day integrate with the auto industry. Accordingly, he pushed for further diversification into those areas.

Autos remained the focus, however, and efforts on their behalf were publicly on display at the 5,400 dealers that comprised Toyota's worldwide network as the new millennium dawned. They were evident as well from the leadership of new president Fujio Cho, who took over when Okuda was elevated to the role of board chairman. Now, he oversees Toyota's latest reinvention. To fight the company's "mid-life crisis," as *Newsweek* called it, he is targeting younger drivers with hotter cars. To grab a piece of the e-commerce potential, he is beefing up the company Web site. And to attract the multi-age "green" crowd, he is offering the gas-and-electric Prius.

It may have once been a simple family-run textile mill. But the Toyota of today remains a very modern company, always ready to try some very fresh ideas.

35

People Express Airlines

Fact File:

✓ Founder: Donald Burr.
✓ Distinction: Made air travel affordable.
✓ Primary products: No-frills, cut-rate airline flights.
✓ Annual revenue: $1 billion at peak.
✓ Number of employees: 3,500 at peak.
✓ Major competitors: American Airlines, Continental Airlines, United Airlines.
✓ Headquarters: Newark, N.J.
✓ Years in existence: 1981-1986.

Before the 1980s, air travel was an expensive luxury. If you absolutely had to haul your family cross-country to visit relatives, you booked the flight and blinked back the tears. If you really wanted a great vacation, you bought the ticket and hoped that you'd still have money left upon landing. And if you truly needed to fly to a trade show or sales meeting, you bit the bullet and prayed that enough business would result to justify the airfare.

In 1981, however, all that changed. Suddenly, a Chicago family of four could visit relatives in Miami for around $350. A vacationer from New York could travel to London for less than $100. And a businesswoman in Los Angeles could fly to a San Francisco meeting for as little as $39.

The reason? People Express, a new kind of airline that set up shop in Newark, N.J., and immediately set the rest of the industry on its ear. Negotiating previously unchartered terrain as a no-frills cut-rate carrier, People attracted people who previously could not afford to fly—along with those who now could justify it more often.

Want to hit Atlanta for the weekend, and don't mind shuffling along with your lunch as if you're at a bus terminal? People Express could fly you from Newark for only $69, while the equivalent ride on Greyhound cost $104 and took 19 hours.

Additionally, People advanced its populist ideals through employees who accepted jobs for much less than competitors paid. Like Internet startups today, the workforce was motivated by the mission—in this case, bringing reasonably priced airfare to the masses. Of course, the stake in company ownership, also offered then didn't hurt.

Not surprisingly, it proved too good to last. Operating on the unstable cusp of the age of airline deregulation, the company's audacious pricing led to massive losses. Administrative cost-cutting further eroded its ability to best the competition, which struck back on its own by also jumping on People's pioneering discount strategies. Employees saw their stock values plummet, until a despised rival finally absorbed the remains. And, in just a few short years, People Express was completely gone from the scene.

As leaders of both their church choir and Sunday school, Donald Burr's parents had always hoped that he would someday enter the ministry. The young Burr developed a taste for commerce instead, and went off to Stanford before earning an M.B.A. at Harvard. Eventually, he parlayed this training into a job with a different kind of high flier: Frank Lorenzo's Texas International Airlines. There, Burr quickly grew personally close to his boss—even serving as the best man at Lorenzo's wedding. He became professionally smitten with the airline business.

Burr was not enamored, though, with Lorenzo's ruthless management style. So, when the industry was deregulated in 1978, he was among those entrepreneurs who began developing plans to launch a new airline. Burr's idea was for a startup that rejected costly amenities in favor of deep discounts that would encourage average consumers to fly more often. He also envisioned a kinder, gentler company that would treat its workforce with dignity and respect—while giving it an unprecedented opportunity to share in any success that ultimately materialized.

Burr and more than a dozen other young executives left Lorenzo's employ in 1980, purchased some old Lufthansa planes, and adopted the name People Express to convey their intended image. With cash of their own bolstered by $24 million raised in the first-ever initial public offering for an airline, they began flying newly repainted jets out of Newark's dilapidated North Terminal the following year to long-ignored cities such as Buffalo, Columbus, and Norfolk. From the start, their daring innovations attracted hordes of appreciative consumers and enthusiastic employees. It also attracted the wrath of Lorenzo—who firmly believed that the idea for a discount airline initially was his, and who greatly resented his one-time friend and protegé for turning it into reality.

Largely because their fixed costs were more or less constrained by expensive infrastructures and ironclad union contracts, even motivated existing operators could not at first duplicate Burr's cut-rate approach. Additional newcomers eventually surfaced with similar concepts, but, like Peoples Express, they soon discovered that there was a lot more to the business than simply attracting employees who were willing to work cheap and a public that wanted to fly for practically nothing. From the time the industry was deregulated through 1986, in fact, some 150 airlines either filed for bankruptcy or completely ceased operations. And at the end of that period, People Express would become the poster child for ways the myriad problems could overrun the vast potential.

None of that was apparent in 1981, however, when the not-yet 40-year-old Burr turned People Express upon the world. Consumers were more than willing to pack their own meals, sit on cold linoleum floors at Newark International Airport, and negotiate endless lines and continuous delays for the chance to fly cross-country for less than $100. Likewise, employees were more than willing to give up standard industry benefits along with a substantial portion of the wages earned by competitors to work in an exciting start-up environment where their opinions were valued and their stock options looked promising.

People's initial bottom-line results appeared quite promising as well. With annual wages only one-half to two-thirds of the industry average, and everyone from baggage handlers to pilots required to perform multiple duties, rock-bottom overhead translated into rock-bottom fares. These helped People fill almost 80 percent of its seats, a remarkably high "load factor" that was markedly better than any of its competitors. More and more cities were added to the schedule as revenues rose, and the once-spotty People Express route map was soon peppered with more than 100 destinations. Among them now were major domestic hubs such as Denver and Chicago, along with popular international locales such as London and Brussels. Additionally, Burr purchased several existing airlines to fuel even more rapid growth. These included Provincetown-Boston, Britt, and Frontier—the latter of which also was coveted by his nemesis, Frank Lorenzo.

As Burr and his lieutenants quickly discovered, however, big-time growth brought big-time problems. When People supplemented its original short-haul flights to under-served airports with discount offerings along already popular routes, entrenched carriers suddenly felt compelled to fight fire with fire. And with rapid route extension necessitating rapid workforce expansion, the cautious hiring practices used from the outset—which carefully screened potential employees to make sure their abilities and temperaments matched those of the company—were tossed aside to simply ensure that enough bodies were available to fill all required jobs.

The result wreaked havoc with an already shaky bottom line. While revenue climbed from $287 million in 1983 to nearly $1 billion in 1985, a $10 million annual profit degenerated into a $28 million annual loss. Consequently, the corporate stock that had been so critical in attracting dedicated workers fell from more than $22 a

About the Author

Howard Rothman has been a retail clerk, vending machine repairman, public opinion pollster, newspaper reporter, magazine editor, advertising agency president, book reviewer, newsletter publisher, business consultant, Internet content provider, television event scout, and book author. He specializes in writing about the impact of technology and progressive management practices on today's ever-evolving business world, and has spoken on these topics at seminars across the nation. A prolific writer for magazines for the past 25 years, he has also written seven books, including the best-selling and critically acclaimed *Companies With A Conscience: Intimate Portraits of Twelve Firms That Make A Difference*, which he co-authored with Mary Scott. He lives with his wife and two daughters in the Colorado city of Centennial, where he is active in the local public school district and an avid bicyclist.